LEADERSHIP
THE SVEN-GÖRAN
ERIKSSON WAY

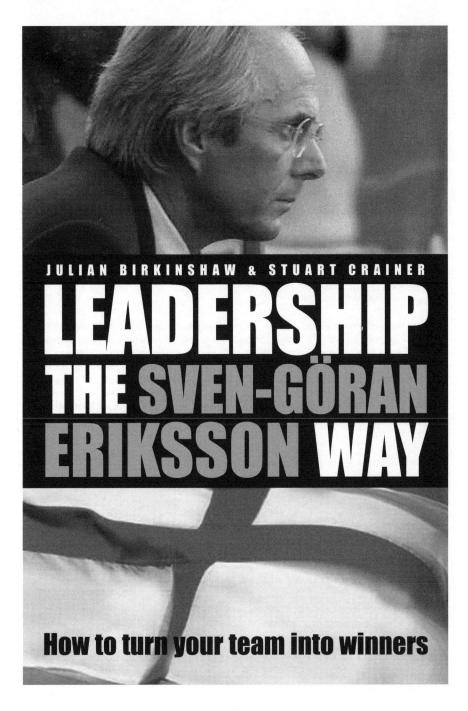

JULIAN BIRKINSHAW & STUART CRAINER

LEADERSHIP
THE SVEN-GÖRAN
ERIKSSON WAY

How to turn your team into winners

CAPSTONE

First published 2002
Second edition 2004
Capstone Publishing Limited (a Wiley company)
The Atrium
Southern Gate
Chichester
West Sussex PO19 8SQ
United Kingdom
http://www.wileyeurope.com

British Library Cataloguing in Publication Data
A CIP catalogue record for this book is available from the British Library

ISBN 1-84112-589-X

10 9 8 7 6 5 4 3 2

Typeset in 10.5/13 pt ITC Garamond by
Sparks Computer Solutions Ltd, Oxford
http://www.sparks.co.uk
Printed and bound by
T.J. International Ltd, Padstow, Cornwall

This book is printed on acid-free paper

Substantial discounts on bulk quantities of Capstone books are available to corporations, professional associations and other organizations.

For details telephone John Wiley & Sons on (+44) 1243 770441, fax (+44)1243 770571 or e-mail CorporateDevelopment@wiley.co.uk

THE AUTHORS

Julian Birkinshaw is Associate Professor of Strategic and International Management at the London Business School. His books include *Entrepreneurship in the Global Firm* and *Inventuring: Why Big Companies Must Think Small*.

Stuart Crainer is co-founder of the consulting and training company, Suntop Media, and editor of *The Financial Times Handbook of Management*. He writes for newspapers and magazines worldwide. Stuart's books include *Generation Entrepreneur* and *Business, the Universe and Everything* (both with Des Dearlove).

CONTENTS

ACKNOWLEDGEMENTS

ooks are team undertakings. The strike force are our publishers in the UK, Capstone, and, in Sweden, Bookhouse Publishing. Thanks go to their Henrik Larssons and Michael Owens, Jan Lapidoth, Mark Allin and John Moseley. Mia Poletto Andersson translated the book into Swedish and checked many of the facts. Jonas Ridderstråle provided funky inspiration.

For Ross, Duncan and Ceira

PREFACE

L eadership is universal. The climber who strides to the front on a tricky mountain ridge is a leader. A factory worker who organizes union activities is a leader. Politicians are leaders. So, too, are soldiers, CEOs, and many, many, more. Leaders touch our lives and, to a greater or lesser extent, we are all leaders.

In this era of mass media entertainment, leaders in the sporting world are among the leadership icons of our times. We are as likely to take our leadership lessons from Michael Jordan as George Bush, from Roy Keane as Bertie Aherne, from David Beckham as Tony Blair. While politics is sullied by cynicism, the sporting world, for all its faults and narrow confines, is perhaps the truest arena for the practice of modern leadership. Little wonder that politicians fall over themselves to associate with sporting leaders. They want to be touched with the same aura of popular appeal and success.

Leadership in the sporting world exists on a perpetual knife edge. There is no hiding place. If Real Madrid's Zinedine Zidane has a bad game, 75,000 people in the stadium and millions more watching in bars and at home know and express their opinion. Sporting history cannot be re-written. There is no second chance, no air brush for the fluffed penalty, no carefully phrased euphemism in the annual report.

The same rules apply to those who lead, manage and coach the sporting performers. If a sports coach makes a bad decision, there is no escape. The media hunt the coach down. Failure is only a bad substitution away.

This is a book about leadership. But the source of its inspiration isn't a charismatic sports star.

This is a book about leadership, but its subject is not the archetypal leadership hero beloved of the movies.

This is a book about a more mature form of leadership practised in a sphere not often noted for the maturity of much of its behaviour.

Leadership the Sven-Göran Eriksson Way examines the leadership style of the England football manager Sven-Göran Eriksson. Our argument is that Eriksson's approach to leadership is important because it brilliantly exemplifies a new approach to leadership which defies conventional and historical stereotypes of how leaders think and behave. Eriksson is a not a tub-thumping bellower of orders. He is no dictator. Instead, he is a modern leadership archetype, a leader we can all learn from.

Eriksson is not alone – simply better known. His approach is typical of a distinctively Scandinavian approach to management and leadership. In *Leadership the Sven-Göran Eriksson Way* we explore the broader practice of this mature form of leadership in companies as diverse as Nokia, Ericsson, IKEA, and Absolut and in leaders such as Jan Carlzon of SAS and Jorma Ollila of Nokia.

Our fascination with the Scandinavian approach to business is long standing. One of us (Julian Birkinshaw) taught at the Stockholm School of Economics and encountered Swedish leadership at first hand. The other (Stuart Crainer) has worked with some of Sweden's leading business thinkers in recent years helping to bring their ideas to a wider audience.

In writing this book some have suggested that we are hostages to fortune. What if the England team play appallingly and Eriksson is pilloried by the excitable English media? Well, it is possible. And, given England's lamentable track record, perhaps probable. But indifferent performances in the short-term are hardly the measure of the man or of a new breed of leadership. Long lasting impact is central to our notion of leadership. One triumphant match does not make for a successful season.

Leadership the Sven-Göran Eriksson Way focuses on Eriksson, but what he stands for and how he behaves has far wider long-term significance. It is the re-invention of leadership and the lessons offered by Eriksson are applicable and useful to leaders no matter what their organization or objectives. *Leadership the Sven-Göran Eriksson Way* is concerned with a leader who has made things happen in every single job he has taken on, but has done so in an understated way. Eriksson's success defies conventional leadership stereotypes. The book will not turn you into a great leader – no book can – but we hope that it opens your eyes to a new form of leadership.

Julian Birkinshaw & Stuart Crainer
March 2004

ENTER SVENNIS

'*Every game has its own story.*'

– *Sven-Göran Eriksson*

1966 and all that

I n 1966 England won the World Cup for the first and only time. They have never looked like winning the most prestigious football trophy on the planet since. Defending their trophy in 1970, they were undone by an injury to their goalkeeper and the high altitude of Mexico City – not to mention inadequate replacements for some of the 1966 team and German persistence. In 1974 they failed to qualify – thanks to an inspired Polish goalkeeper and more inadequate replacements for fading heroes. In 1978 they again failed to qualify. In 1982 they scored quickly and then faded gently away, their only world class player, Kevin Keegan, appearing for a matter of minutes – long enough to miss a crucial chance. In 1986 England performed gamely before being beaten by Diego Maradona. In 1990, they reached the semi-final. It took some miraculous comebacks and a change of tactics (brought about by the team rather than the manager) to get them that far. In 1994 they failed to qualify. Then, in 1998, they once again stumbled after looking set to make progress.

And then in 2002, under Sven-Göran Eriksson, England's young team reached the quarter finals. Whether this was yet another English failure is open to debate. What can be said is that England underperformed in their final game and never quite convinced the world – or themselves – that they believed they could win.

For the English, reading this litany of under achievement is a depressing experience. The depression, however, appears to be only momentary. When it comes to football, the English suspend normal mental functions. Their memories have the longevity of those of goldfish. And so, the English expect their team to win the World Cup no matter where it is held, who is in their team or who they are playing. When the World Cup is held in Germany in 2006, all of England will expect the England captain David Beckham to hold the trophy in his hands.

The decades of dismal performances are overlooked. The fact that England have only won the World Cup with home advantage is completely ignored. Throw in the fact that the English team also attracts a significant number of hooligans and you have a thoroughly depressing spectre; mindlessness and forgetfulness.

At least the Scots have realistic expectations – they expect to lose – and dedicate themselves to alcoholic pleasures and exposing their genitals to foreigners untutored in what Scots wear under their kilts.

The English football team and its supporters has no such saving grace.

Little wonder then that the job of manager of the English football team has long been a poisoned chalice. Success has proved as elusive as the expectations are immense. The English manager is on a hiding to nothing, drowning in the goldfish bowl of expectation. It is like being made CEO of a loss-making company in a decaying market with indifferent staff and plummeting morale and being expected to deliver double digit growth tomorrow while cutting costs. 'The days of the England manager lasting six or eight years are long gone. It is so instant now. Here you go, it's your job, get on with it and you had better be successful,' reflects Kevin Keegan, who quickly found the job too much.[1]

Given this mission impossible, managers have come and gone in pursuit of the English dream.

The success story was the unlikely figure of Sir Alf Ramsey (manager from 1963 until 1974). Ramsey managed the 1966 team. He spoke in an unfeasibly refined accent, had little time for the media, and, for the most part, resembled a slightly portly bank manager. Nevertheless, he was blessed by a cohort of world-class players from which he selected Bobby Moore as a natural leader. Ramsey left – treated shoddily – when he found it difficult to replace the greats of 1966.

At this point things went downhill fast. The English Football Association (FA) selected Don Revie, then the manager of Leeds United, as the new manager. Revie was the obvious choice. The alternative was the outspoken and eccentric Brian Clough. Revie was dour and serious, but had turned Leeds from no-hopers into the English champions. The club had few footballing admirers –they were never pretty – but they were successful. For a shrewd club manager, Revie proved inexplicably clueless when in charge of the national team. After only 29 games he departed to coach in the United Arab Emirates, footballing purdah.

Then came Ron Greenwood, an ageing but safe pair of hands. Greenwood stabilised things but England still lost. He was followed by another successful English club manager, Bobby Robson, who managed to lead England to the heady heights of a semi-final place before he, too, left, exhausted by press expectations and continual sniping.

Graham Taylor, another club manager, followed. Patently intelligent and decent, Taylor was a dismal failure. His selections were, at times, bizarre, displaying a preference for limited journeymen over players with international ability. Terry Venables, the former Barcelona coach, added much needed flair and tactical coherence, but then left to fight a legal case. A former England star, Glenn Hoddle, entered the fray and built up expectations until they were dashed once again. Hoddle departed after an ill-advised comment to the media. Luckily another English playing legend was on hand, Kevin Keegan. The former European footballer of the year brought enthusiasm but admitted that tactics were a mystery. He left in autumn 2000 immediately after a dismal, damp defeat to Germany, the last game played at the original Wembley stadium where Bobby Moore had paraded the Jules Rimet trophy 34 years previously.

So what does this long and lengthening litany of disappointment add up to? What can we learn? Well, first, no-one has a right to success – not even someone with three lions on their shirt. Second, continuity is important. There has been little continuity since Ramsey's departure in style, tactics, outlook or leadership. Third, as England have struggled they have become more and more insular. Their performances appear constricted by history, contained by their feelings of disappointment and fruitless optimism. They have played with the heavy burden of history on their shoulders and have not had the leadership to set themselves free.

When in Rome

While sodden England were losing to Germany and Keegan was rushing towards resignation, the champions of Italy, Lazio, were contemplating life in the European Champions League. At the end of the previous season the Rome-based club had staged one of the great comebacks. With seven matches to go they had trailed nine points behind the formidable Juventus of Torino. Undaunted, they stormed back to win only the second championship – 'scudetto' – in their history. Their previous triumph had been 26 years before.

Unwilling to rest on their laurels, Lazio had spent the summer acquiring a host of big name players at considerable expense. The light blue shirts of the Italian champions were now worn by the likes of Alessandro Nesta, Italy's finest defender; the silkily skilled Czech Pavlo Nedved; the Chilean Marcelo Salas; the Argentine Hérnan Crespo; the indecently boyish Simone Inzaghi and many more.

The man who had brought the league and cup double to Lazio was a quietly spoken Swede, Sven-Göran Eriksson.

As Kevin Keegan retreated to his home, out of reach of the prying media, Eriksson's was one of the names in the minds of the seven-man panel created by the English Football Association to find the next manager of England. Indeed, the FA's lack of forward planning meant that he was pretty much the only name on the list. (The FA had been caught out before – when Glenn Hoddle resigned the FA had no one else in mind apart from Keegan.)

In some ways the FA's immediate targeting of Eriksson was a fashion statement. After the success of Arsene Wenger at Arsenal, English teams have recruited coaches from other countries with increasing enthusiasm and some success – the Frenchman Jean Tigana was at Fulham, Gerrard Houllier at Liverpool, the Italian Claudio Ranieri at Chelsea. Cynically one could say that the FA was simply following the pattern. More positively it could be said that the FA and its then CEO Adam Crozier were anxious to cast aside the baggage of the past and to have a new approach to and perspective on the England job.

Eriksson did not fit the usual English solution to their perennial problem. He had never coached in England. Though once lined up to coach the English club Blackburn Rovers while at Sampdoria, he had uncharacteristically pulled out of the deal. (The suspicion is that the urbane Eriksson with his mastery of languages and stylish suits would have found damp and unfashionable Blackburn a sizeable cultural challenge after life in Genova.)

Nor had Eriksson been a great player. In footballing terms, Eriksson was not fit to lace the boots of the likes of previous English managers like Keegan and Hoddle or, indeed, Robson and Ramsey who also played international football.

As a player, Sven-Göran Eriksson was distinctly limited. Indeed, his entire early background was unremarkable. He was born in Torsby, in 1948, the son of a truck driver. Torsby is in Varmland, an area, in the centre of Sweden near to the Norwegian border. Even now

Eriksson is wont to say 'Well, I come from Varmland' after giving a cryptically simple reply to a media question. Oslo is the nearest big city – 200 kilometres away. Torsby is a small town in a country with a small population; ordinary, dedicatedly normal. The town's major attraction is, somewhat strangely, its Finnish Cultural Centre. If you find Torsby on a map you will see that it is surrounded by blankness.

Eriksson made his debut for the team of his birthplace aged just seventeen. Torsby were in the fourth division. 'When I put him in for his first game there were a lot of complaints. But after the game and the next day there were none,' the club manager Sven-Ake Olsson later recalled. 'He is a very ordinary guy, well brought up, polite and calm, never any outbursts of emotions. He always thinks first, then speaks. It's in his blood. He does not get excited easily.'[2] With the polite, self-contained Eriksson playing at right back Torsby were soon promoted. It remains the greatest achievement in the club's history.

Eriksson's playing career never reached the peaks. In Swedish terms he was a footnote footballer, a name but never a star. His career ended in 1975 through an injury he sustained while playing for Karlskoga, a small, heavily industrial town in the Swedish second division.

The career coach

Eriksson then joined Degerfors, in the Swedish third division, as assistant to its manager, Tord Grip. Grip had met Eriksson while he was playing at Karlskoga. It was Grip who suggested that Eriksson should pursue a career in coaching. It was to be the start of a long-term relationship.

Grip left to work with the national team after a season and Eriksson was left in charge as the club coach. It was 1976; Eriksson was 28. Eriksson led Degerfos into the second division and then, in 1979, he became coach of IFK Gothenburg, one of the biggest clubs in Sweden. Eriksson turned Gothenburg into a European force. It didn't happen overnight and, early on in his time with the club, dissatisfied Gothenburg fans were wont to advise that Eriksson should be sent back to the woods where he came from. He didn't go back. Together they won the Swedish Cup, the championship and the UEFA Cup in 1982. In the final Gothenburg demolished the German team Hamburg, 4–0 (1–0 at home; 3–0 away).

In 1982 he moved to Benfica of Portugal where he won the championship and cup. But these were routine victories. Benfica take success as their right.

Eriksson's success in Sweden and Portugal prompted growing interest from Italian clubs. Eriksson was marketable and, in 1984, his Italian jobs began as manager of Roma. In the first season, Roma struggled to seventh in the league. He led them to the Italian Cup and almost to the summit of Serie A – Roma lost the title to Juventus by a mere two points.

Italian football club owners are not renowned for their patience. This was not good enough. Eriksson was fired but speedily became manager of Fiorentina. This proved an ill-starred move – the first and only in his career – and Eriksson sought to regroup by returning to Benfica. It worked. Eriksson's magic touch returned and he led Benfica to the 1990 European Cup Final, though they lost to Milan.

In 1992 Eriksson returned to Italy with Sampdoria of Genova where he won the Italian Cup. The Sampdoria experience was a formative one. The club performed less well under Eriksson than it had done in the years immediately previous when the club had enjoyed success in Europe and in the domestic league. But Eriksson's position was seriously undermined by the need to sell a galaxy of the club's stars for financial reasons – Ruud Gullitt, David Platt, Clarence Seedorf and others were off-loaded. Eriksson was then faced with the challenge of keeping the club going and of motivating and marshalling the demotivated and lesser skilled players who remained. He did so. When he departed, the club went into freefall and languished amid the also-rans of Serie B until promotion in 2003.

In 1997 he joined Lazio, taking over from the Italian goalkeeping legend Dino Zoff who had stepped into the breach after Zdenek Zeman's departure from the club during the previous season. (The ins and outs of Italian football make the jobs of CEOs and politicians, even Italian politicians, seem positively secure.) At Lazio, he won the Italian Cup, Italian Super Cup, European Cup Winners Cup and UEFA Super Cup before crowning his Italian stay with the Serie A title and Italian Cup in 2000.

On October 31 2000, Sven-Göran Eriksson signed up to become the new manager of England. The ever faithful Tord Grip, who had been with Eriksson in Italy, was signed as his assistant.

The initial idea was that Eriksson would continue with Lazio until the following year and the end of his contract. This did not work. Lazio struggled. Eriksson's attention was – rightly or wrongly – thought to be elsewhere. On January 9 2001 he resigned as Lazio coach – after the team had been beaten by struggling Napoli – and took up the reins with England. 'It is very bad news and a very difficult day for us. Lazio owed Eriksson a lot,' said Sergio Cragnotti, the club's owner.[3] Owners of Italian football clubs are rarely so glowing in their praise.

All was not automatically sweetness and light. His appointment was far from universally celebrated. Many in the British media and the football world bemoaned the appointment of a foreigner as national football coach.

'What have we done? The French have a Frenchman, the Germans have a German and the Italians have an Italian,' said a somewhat be-mused Jack Charlton on Eriksson's appointment. Charlton, a hero of England's 1966 triumph, overlooked the fact that he, an Englishman, led Ireland to their greatest footballing triumphs. He also chose to overlook the long tradition of countries appointing foreign coaches – usually when national coaches had proved not to be up to the task. (Witness Roy Hodgson, an Englishman in Switzerland; Sepp Piontek, a German leading the Danes; and László Kubala, a Hungarian, who coached Spain.)

Others echoed Charlton's thoughts. John Barnwell, CEO of the League Managers' Association commented: 'We favoured an English-man, and our thinking remains clear. International football is about pitting your nation's skill against another nation's skill. If you don't have the necessary skills, you have to work at developing it through your players, coaches and managers. We stand by our opinion. No other major country has a foreign coach. In Greece, it's even part of their constitution that they don't have one.'[4] (Even so, the Greek team which was soon to play Eriksson's England had a constitutionally de-batable German at the helm.)

The country which invented football now had a foreign coach. Eriksson needed to prove himself – and prove himself quickly.

Making a mark

There are a profusion of books which offer guides to what to do during your first days in a particular job. Political leaders are appraised on their first 100 days in office. Of course, in reality there is no magical timescale. An initially successful leader can screw things up completely on the 101st day. But the point is an important one: the leader has to make a mark from the very start. The leader has to set the tone from the beginning.

And herein lies the first leadership lesson from Sven-Göran Eriksson. He proved immediately adept at making a mark. He led from the very first day. His approach is worthy of emulation. For the first-time leader or the newly appointed leader Eriksson's lessons were:

- **Distance yourself from the past.** Carefully and delicately, Eriksson made it clear that he had no associations with the past. The past really was a foreign country. This was a new beginning, an opportunity for people to shine once again – or to slide into history. 'Any football team needs continuity and six managers in ten years provides its own answer. If you're happy, you don't change the manager,' he noted.[5] 'He's come in with no bias towards any club or player. There's no history with the press or anyone else. Everyone knew from day one there was no agenda: if you were good enough you were in. Everyone would be treated in exactly the same way,' the FA's Adam Crozier reflected.[6] Some would say it's easy for an outsider to rise above politics and in-fighting, but that sooner rather than later they will be dragged into the political mire. The reality is that it doesn't have to be like that. The best leaders work hard at escaping the poison of organisational politics. Their only agenda is success.
- **Survey the scene.** His first move was simple enough: to watch football, lots of football. In a much publicised progress around the football stadia of England, Grip and Eriksson proceeded to watch every match they could. (Eriksson reportedly managed to attend 22 matches in five weeks.) Eriksson was applauded to his seat on some occasions – an experience which can be filed under bizarre. Curiously, the football supporting public welcomed the

Swede with open arms. The fickleness and misfortunes of the past appeared forgotten.

- **Identify the problem areas.** For reasons which had bewildered previous coaches and the English media, the English team had trouble finding a left-footed player. This seems incredible. After years of the best money can buy in Italy, Eriksson found himself coaching a nation populated entirely by right-footed footballers. Miraculously, Eriksson found a left-footed player no-one had previously encountered (Chris Powell of Charlton Athletic) within weeks of getting the job. The problem was not exactly solved, but it was quickly put on ice.

- **Accentuate the positive.** Eriksson was relentlessly positive. 'I was very lucky, I came at the right moment,' he said when interviewed. 'There are many good young players. The first thing is to pick the squad, make the squad come together and start talking about going to the World Cup 2002. And if there is anyone who does not believe in that, they can go home at once, because being negative, not believing that we have the possibility, I don't like that.'[7]

- **Make initial gains and then build on them.** Herein lies the simple secret of any leader's success. Start winning from the start. And, even if you are not making dramatic wins make it appear as if you are. Strike while the winds of change remain in the air. Otherwise, they have a nasty habit of disappearing as people embrace the existing status quo with ever greater enthusiasm.

Qualified success

Eriksson's first game was a routine 3–0 victory in a friendly game against Spain on 28 February 2001. England, for a change, performed as if the players actually knew each other. (Coincidentally, the game was played at Villa Park where Eriksson had led Lazio to victory in the 1999 European Cup Winners Cup Final.)

Then began the serious work of qualifying for the World Cup. A poor start to the campaign (home defeat to Germany, draw with Finland) meant that everything came down to a critical away fixture against Germany. Already this game has gone down into English footballing folklore. (And Swedish folklore as well – more Swedes watched the

England/Germany game than the simultaneous Sweden/Macedonia match.) Eriksson's greatest achievement has not been qualifying for the World Cup having inherited a dispirited poorly performing side. For every Englishman, England and Eriksson's towering achievement is already in the history books: Germany 1 England 5.

For the English, Germany remains the arch footballing enemy. In the decades following 1966 the Germans have ritually beaten England – in Mexico in 1970 in extra time; in Italy on penalties for a place in the World Cup final; and at Wembley in 1996 on penalties. The English perception is not so much that losing to Germany is bad but it is the manner of the defeats – England beaten time and time again through German persistence, professionalism, sheer teutonic efficiency. It is not that the English are wildly creative. They would simply like to win.

Away to Germany in Munich, the English team came of age. It was the first time England had won a World Cup qualifier against Germany or beaten them on German soil in any match in nearly 70 years. True, the Germans were terrible, but England played with a style and self-belief which was remarkable – especially considering the lacklustre incompetence demonstrated by England in their previous meeting.

'In terms of the German game, all of us said, we won't come here to lose this game. We will take a chance and win it,' says Eriksson. 'And there are many positive players in this team. And maybe I changed that … some of the older players had been there a lifetime, we took them away, and said, Ashley Cole, he is good, 19, if he is the best left back in the country, let him play. And the same for a couple of others, young, fresh up here [in the head], they are not afraid of Germany so I think it is a very positive atmosphere.'[8]

In September 2001 after England had beaten Germany 5–1 the newspapers struck a slightly different tone than the xenophobia displayed on Eriksson's appointment. The *News of the World* headline was: 'Sven's the real deal. Eriksson is our superhero as five goal lions roar.' The *Daily Express* reflected: 'Put into context this win represents one of the greatest performances by an England team. Eriksson has done so much to establish this new sense of pride and purpose, to get the best out of the outstanding individual talents at his disposal.' (On Eriksson's appointment the *Express* offered a less positive summation: 'Ultimately, the designer FA now has its designer manager.')

Eriksson, inevitably, was more cautionary. 'People are talking about the German game a lot,' he said. 'It was a fantastic result, but I don't think we deserved to win 5–1. We were a bit lucky. We scored all our opportunities. In life you must be lucky also. We deserved to win, but 5–1 no.'[9]

The optimism lasted. England strode on to beat Albania (with some difficulty) and then, dramatically, stricken by nerves, to clinch a draw with Greece after being twice behind with virtually the last kick of the match to qualify for the World Cup finals.

As a result, Eriksson went into the 2002 World Cup with a wave of goodwill behind him. England's defeat of Germany, David Beckham's dramatic equaliser against Greece and Eriksson's tabloid-featured relationship with TV celebrity Ulrika Johnson meant that Eriksson was lionised as quiet but persuasive, cool but passionate.

The World Cup proved a mixed bag. Triumph over Argentina was surrounded by indifferent performances against Sweden and Nigeria. A convincing win over Denmark was followed by elimination against Brazil, the tournament's best team by a considerable margin.

Eriksson emerged largely unscathed. Only the suspicion that he was not passionate (or English) enough to deliver Henry V style oratory at half-time in the Brazil game counted against him.

And then, moving speedily on, England qualified for the 2004 European Championships. Along the way they displayed their characteristic mix of incompetence, brilliance, bull-dog spirit, media disasters and loutishness.

Yet, as we write early in 2004, the feelgood factor surrounding Eriksson largely remains.

Notes

1 Woolnough, Brian, *Poisoned Chalice,* Ebury, 2000.
2 'Hometown hero', www.sportsillustrated.cnn.com, November 4 2000.
3 'Eriksson quits', www.sportsillustrated.cnn.com, 9 January 2001.
4 Glanville, Brian, 'England and foreigners', www.hinduonnet.com.
5 Anthony, Andrew, 'Svengland', *The Observer,* 5 August 2001.
6 Campbell, Denis, 'The history man', *The Observer,* 13 January 2002.

7 Interview with George Yip of London Business School, 28 September 2001.

8 Interview with George Yip of London Business School, 28 September 2001.

9 Interview with George Yip of London Business School, 28 September 2001.

2

SWEDES 2 TURNIPS 1

'Pound for pound, Sweden probably has more good managers than any other country.'

– former GE CEO, Jack Welch

The Swedish way

I n 1992 the England manager Graham Taylor led England to the European championships in Sweden. England's performances were dismal. Players of indifferent ability played out of position – and still played indifferently. One of England's best players, John Barnes, was injured in the build-up to the tournament. Arguably, Taylor's greatest mistake was to substitute the captain Gary Lineker at a time when England were hunting for goals. England lost 2–1 to Sweden. Next day's tabloid headline has become legendary: Swedes 2 Turnips 1.

Ten years later, a Swede manages the England team.

Sven-Göran Eriksson epitomises an entire way of thinking and working that is quintessentially Swedish. His responses to questions are always measured, tactful and direct. He is not given to lengthy speeches or emotional outbursts. He never seems to lose his cool. On listening to Eriksson, the uninitiated observer might even be tempted to call his approach boring, lacking in passion or simplistic. But the fact is, this style works – it works for the England manager, and it has worked for generations of Swedish executives.

Understand Sweden and you begin to understand Eriksson.

Sweden is an unusual country in many respects. It has only nine million inhabitants, spread over a country that is larger in land mass than the entire British Isles. As recently as the late nineteenth century it was primarily a farming economy, but it industrialised quickly through the innovative genius of people like Alfred Nobel and Lars Magnus Ericsson. Industrial companies like Alfa Laval, Asea and Ericsson sprang up and quickly established an international presence in the Scandinavian region, and into Russia. Commercial success led to further economic growth and the 'Swedish model' began to emerge – a social democratic government committed to full employment, generous social policies, and powerful labour unions (with surprisingly amicable connections to wealthy industrialists like the Wallenberg family).

All of this is relevant because it helps to explain the Swedish way of working. The Swedes are a surprisingly homogeneous group. There is a strong work ethic. They have strongly held beliefs about equality. They feel they have to stick together in a big unfriendly world. There is a strong desire to fit in and conform to the norms and expectations of those around them.

Research has examined the ways that Sweden's national culture differs from that of other countries.[1] The first key attribute, which Sweden shares with Japan among others, is a strong *collectivist* culture – a belief in the importance of the group or the team ahead of the individual. Britain and America are the opposite – they have a highly individualistic culture, where kids learn from a young age to stand up for themselves, to seek out attention and to compete with their peers. In Sweden, the reverse is true. Kids are expected to be average (though the Swedish word *lagom* sounds a lot better than average), and the school system dampens down any naturally competitive instincts they may have. In Sweden there is a joke about a clothing size called 'extra medium' which is supposed to fit the entire nation.

'He [Eriksson] is the typical Swedish leader,' says cultural diversity expert Fons Trompenaars. 'We have looked at the enormously decentralised multinational firms. They are empowerers. Swedish leadership is about consensus. It is about harmony. They hate conflict. It would be interesting to find out why the Swedish style seems to gel with English football which is full of aggression and a sense of fair play. English football is very opportunistic, big jumps to the goal and hit it.'[2]

A second attribute is the lack of hierarchy, or what academics have called *power distance* (the level of inequality between individuals in society). One of us worked at the Stockholm School of Economics, the leading Swedish business school. The contrast with British academia was unmistakable. In UK universities the professors, in their chairs, sit at the top, followed by readers, senior lecturers, and lecturers. Below them are the students – the undergraduates, and the graduate students. Graduate students, in particular, are used to working as full-time slaves to their supervisors, fulfilling their bidding for perhaps five years before gaining their Ph.Ds. Hierarchy rules.

Academia Swedish style is a little different. On the first day, there was a departmental meeting. The professor opined about something vaguely important – a new programme they were thinking of putting on. Then a graduate student answered back. 'I disagree,' was his opening statement, and he went on to put forward an alternative point of view, which led to a lively discussion of the pros and cons of the different options. Of course, this was nothing unusual to the rest of the group, all Swedes. They were accustomed to a system in which everyone was free to challenge everyone else. It was just a bit of a shock to an Englishman accustomed to a very different type of boss-subordinate relationship.

Much the same level of informality and openness can be found in the boardrooms of Swedish companies. If you try and talk to a CEO in the UK or US you have to get past a protective secretary and a PR minder. The CEO is likely to be highly elusive. CEOs do not answer the phone. They have secretaries who do that. They then recline, put the phone onto 'speak' and pontificate. In Sweden we have called CEOs directly and got straight through, not a secretary in sight, just two people talking.

Translate this to the English football team and it means that the team has access to Eriksson and he to the team. There is a climate of openness.

There are two other elements that are typically used to characterise the Swedish culture. One is that Swedes are much more in touch with *feminine* values like nurturing, caring and supporting, than the more *masculine* societies like the US and the UK. You see this in child care, where fathers are encouraged to take six months paternity leave. And you also see it in team situations, where the manager (male or female) tries to understand and support the troubled employee. As we shall see, Swedes are natural teamworkers.

The final element of cultural make-up is the Swedes' high level of *tolerance of uncertainty* – the ability to ride the rollercoaster of life without fear of crashing or falling off. This is especially useful if you are a football coach. In addition, this has a lot of important consequences in the world of business, because it makes Swedes less resistant to change, more able to accommodate new ways of thinking, and more tolerant of foreigners. It also manifests itself in the rather informal way of doing business in Sweden. When one of us agreed to move to Sweden from Canada for a job, no employment contract was offered – a handshake and a verbal agreement were sufficient, at least to the Swedish employer.

The Swedish national culture, then, is different in many important respects from what is the norm elsewhere in Europe and in the UK. As always, it is possible to pick out broad differences in national traits, and we can speculate on the reasons why they turned out that way. But the important question is whether this actually makes a difference – one way or the other – to effective management. Does the cultural background of Sven-Göran Eriksson make a difference to how he leads, coaches and manages? Does the fact that he is Swedish matter? The answer is an unequivocal 'yes'.

Consider a few facts about Sweden and Swedish companies.

- Sweden has more large companies per head of population than any other country in the world. Many of them are still independent world leaders in their chosen sectors – Ericsson in mobile infrastructure, Sandvik in tooling, Electrolux in white goods. Some of them, including Volvo cars and Astra, have recently been bought up by foreigners – a sure sign that they are valued overseas. And importantly, the Swedes often end up running the merged company. ABB, a merger of Sweden's Asea and Switzerland's Brown Boveri, is headquartered in Zurich, but three of four CEOs since the merger have been Swedes.
- Sweden has a long and impressive tradition of industrial innovation. Sandvik was the first company to commercialise Bessemer steel production. Lars Magnus Ericsson invented the telephone switch. Such everyday items as the zipper, the safety match, and dynamite were all invented by Swedish innovators. More recently Swedish companies have been responsible for a number of *management* innovations. The cellular manufacturing model was pioneered by Volvo in its Kalmar factory. In the late 1980s Electrolux and SKF were the first truly transnational companies in which foreign subsidiaries were given global strategic roles. Scandinavian companies also led the way in decentralising. IKEA is an exemplar of the networked organisation – a web with no centre. Then there is ABB with its decidedly ambiguous – if not confusing – matrix structure.
- Sweden has been labelled the most 'future ready' country in the world in the IMD/WEF annual competitiveness rankings. There is a highly-sophisticated broadband infrastructure – enough to put even the most wired parts of Britain to shame. Seventy per cent of people have Internet access. Mobile telephone penetration is close to 100 per cent.

   And after Silicon Valley, Stockholm (or rather Kista, a suburb north of Stockholm) is widely recognised as one of the leading high-tech clusters in the world, right up there with Cambridge's Silicon Fen. Over the last couple of years leading IT companies including Microsoft, Nortel, Intel and Oracle all put R&D investments into Stockholm, as a means of tapping into the latest thinking in the world of the mobile Internet. Steve Ballmer, president of Microsoft, said in 2000: 'I know no better place to base our mobile telephony business. Stockholm is the centre of mobility.' And *Newsweek* ran a cover story in February 2000 called 'Shining Stockholm' with the subheading, 'Sweden is the most wired and wireless nation in Europe, and Internet fever is energising its capital, from business to the arts'.

Sweden also rates highly in business start-ups and entrepreneurship. Venture capital investment grew 200 per cent between 1995 and 1999, more than any other country in the world. And Sweden also tops the table of high-growth start-ups, according to the Global Entrepreneurship Monitor produced by London Business School.

- In addition, Sweden punches above its weight in the worlds of design and entertainment. It is a creative economy. 'Like Finland, Sweden is technology-driven,' reflects Alexander Bard, the Swedish author, lecturer, TV talk show host, government adviser, record producer, songwriter, artist and composer of over 80 Scandinavian top 40 hit records. 'Being an engineer is the ultimate in social status in Sweden. Being a 50-year old engineer is something we dream of! But, at the same time, pop culture and fashion are taken very seriously here in a way they aren't elsewhere.'[3]

Creatives like Bard find fertile ground in high-tech, fashion conscious Stockholm. It is the same elsewhere in the country. Creatives rule.

Take the world of furniture for example. IKEA's armchairs and cupboards may not be anyone's idea of a fashion statement today, but that's only because the whole mass-market furniture industry has adopted the Swedish retailer's model. IKEA – a lean, networked organisation which has established itself globally in the stylish, but cheap, furniture market. The brain-child of the reclusive and occasionally controversial Ingvar Kamprad, IKEA remains privately owned – if it became publicly owned it would be valued at some $12 billion. IKEA's secret is a labyrinthian network – 2000 suppliers in 70 countries – which enables it to keep prices at an average 20 per cent below those of other furniture retailers.

There is more. In music everyone knows about ABBA, Ace of Base, Roxette and Robyn. Less well known is Max Martin, the Swede who is responsible for penning all of of Britney Spears' hit records. When you look at the complete inability of French or German popular artists to make it on a world stage, the success of many Swedish artists is all the more impressive.

- Swedish management itself is recognised and respected. Indeed, the Swedes have been setting the managerial agenda for decades. During the 1980s, Jan Carlzon, CEO of the airline SAS, proclaimed 'All business is show business', and actually made customer service work. He used it as a vehicle for turning the airline around.

  For a time, with a neat line in phrase-making and a great story to tell, Carlzon was hardly out of the business magazines. Business, he said, was all about 'moments of truth' when customers interacted with employees. Get the moments of truth right, and success was sure to follow. Carlzon's book was an international bestseller selling three million copies.

  After Carlzon left SAS and the company's halo slipped a little, Swedish role models were thin on the ground for a number of years. In recent years, however, there has been a steady stream of Swedish corporate benchmarks. (Carlzon has not been left behind – he has successfully re-invented himself as a high-tech venture capitalist and consultant.)

Among the country's success stories is Absolut vodka, one of the most bizarre and unusual success stories of our branded times. Absolut has become the fifth largest spirits brand in the world and the number one imported vodka in the United States with 60 per cent of the market. Such is the brand's success that Richard Lewis' *Absolut Book: The Absolut Vodka Advertising Story* reportedly sold 150,000 copies. Books about state-run former monopolies are not usually so popular.

At the time of Absolut's inception – the end of the 1970s and the beginning of the 1980s – the generic strategy to crack the spirits market was to have a big bottle with a Russian name, suitably detailed heritage and a large label with crests and crowns. Absolut deliberately did the opposite. In many ways the Absolut team's initial ignorance of the spirits industry was their greatest asset.

Sweden's economy has also grown impressively over the last decade. Its average GDP growth of around 3 per cent since 1997 puts it ahead of Germany, France and the UK. The country's revival is such that it is easy to forget that its currency was devalued at the beginning of the 1990s and that it has had a social democratic government for all but nine of the last 68 years. Sweden has re-invented itself without shedding its long-term commitments to taxation and welfare. (Swedish corporate tax is set at 28 per cent and tax still accounts for 52 per cent of GDP.)

The art of Swedish management

The history of business and leadership is littered with ways of working that were picked up in one place and adopted overseas. In the UK the dominant influence has been American. From the tools of Scientific Management in the pre-war years, through the creation of the multi-divisional organisation form, to the more recent obsessions with re-engineering and value-based management, the influence of American gurus and American practices is omnipresent. But there have been other influences as well. In the 1980s the West embraced Japanese management. There were useful techniques like just-in-time manufacturing, quality circles, and constant improvement. And also rather more dubious practices like company songs, and 250-year plans (Matsushita has one of these).

In the UK, there have also been influences from Germany and France, though the average Englishman would only ever admit this through gritted teeth. Unlike American and Japanese practices, there has been no widespread adoption of the 'continental model'. But if the economic statistics are even half-right, there is still a productivity gap between Britain and the rest of continental Europe. And there are world-leading companies that deserve a closer look – like Renault, LVMH, Siemens and Hoechst. So the benchmarking studies have been done. The foreign executives have been hired. And bit by bit, the management models of Germany and France have found their way into the British boardroom and onto the shopfloor.

Swedish management comes with none of the baggage of the German and French models. It is unthreatening. It is polite. Think of Sven-Göran Eriksson. And it is an approach to management that is already relatively familiar, with its emphasis on things like empowerment, teamwork, and consensus-based decision making.

This may explain why there was little interest in Scandinavian role models during the early 1990s when downsizing and re-engineering held sway – corporations didn't want their consciences pricked by touchy-feely Swedes who treated employees like drinking buddies.

All of this is not to suggest that the Swedes are paragons of camaraderie. Like most stereotypes, the image of highly motivated, hard working and contented Swedes is only partly true. Swedish companies have a track record in managing their human resources in innovative ways – they were champions of team working and employee participation long before they became the height of managerial fashion. Even so, it is easy to overstate this. 'There is a belief that we are better at caring for people, that we have a more humanitarian view of business. I think it is vastly exaggerated,' says Jan Lapidoth, an SAS vice-president under Jan Carlzon, who now runs the media group Bookhouse Publishing in Stockholm. 'More significant is the fact that we are a very stable political society and a fairly homogeneous society. We have solved our problems through negotiation. Historically, there has been little unrest but the counter to this is that often without a crisis you don't achieve advancement.'

Indeed, the Swedish business culture shares some characteristics with that of the Japanese – the Swedes have sometimes been labelled the 'Japanese of Europe'. Saving face is important and, rather than direct frontal attack, they prefer a more obtuse and subtle approach. For this reason, Swedes remain largely immune to the quick-fix-gurus who promise to cure all known organisation ills at one seminar. 'New ideas are better stated in quite general and vague terms initially, in order to invite others into the process,' note Ingalill Holmberg and Staffan Åkerblom of the Stockholm School of Economics. 'Swedes are generally very suspicious of readymade ideas or solutions. It is also a matter of ownership. If a Swede has not been involved in the generation process, no one should take for granted that they will be involved in the implementation.'

Holmberg and Åkerblom's extensive research into leadership and culture in Sweden found that Sweden achieved the highest international ranking for non-assertiveness.

This does not mean that they are pushovers – just that they prefer simplicity and straightforwardness to pointless prevarication. The Swedes have an appetite for brevity and avoiding expensive legal fees. This was most notably seen in the merger that created the industrial giant ABB. Negotiations were conducted in secret. When the boards were shown the draft agreement for the first time, some directors had no idea a merger was afoot. They had an hour to read the papers. The entire process was extraordinarily quick. Due diligence was notable for its absence as the company's indefatigable leader Percy Barnevik pushed to clinch the deal. When a draft agreement was generated, Barnevik read it out line by line in front of both negotiating teams. Objections were ironed out on the spot. If voices weren't raised, it was taken as agreed. 'We had to be fast; there could be no leakage; we could not have lawyers around; we had to trust each other,' Barnevik reflected. When the merger was announced on 10 August 1987, the corporate world was stunned by its suddenness.

Even so, Nike's call 'Just do it' does not quite work in Sweden. It is recounted that the typical Swedish edict is 'See what you can do about it'. Forget command and control. The Scandinavian leader is decidedly anti-authoritarian. Highly personal and practical theories, such as coaching and empowering, find fertile ground. And the media presentation of business leaders is also notably different. While American CEOs become corporate touchstones, icons; their Swedish counterparts like Kurt Hellström of Ericsson or Leif Johansson of Volvo remain studiously anonymous.

Listen to the views of Conor McKechnie who has worked for two years in Sweden as a communications consultant: 'My experience has shown me that the Swedish way can lead to genuine commitment, engagement and passion in a company's employees. With a focus on inclusion and communicative leadership, Swedish companies, although perhaps not always the quickest to make decisions, are better at making the right ones and successfully implementing them.'[4]

The Swedish model, in other words, affords us with a new perspective on management and leadership. It is far more accessible than the French or German models, and it is practiced by people who speak English almost as well as the English. We are not predicting a wave of enthusiasm for Swedish management to match the early 1980s when all things Japanese were celebrated. Rather, we see the Swedish model – with Sven-Göran Eriksson as its examplar – as a new way of making sense of a very old approach to management – that you should believe in and respect the ability of every individual who works for you.

Swedish management and leadership, in other words, offers something both different and effective. And the bottom line is simple – whether you are running a business or coaching a soccer team – it works.

Cultural differences between countries

Cultural stereotyping is hard to avoid – the brash, assertive American; the disciplined, humourless German; the reserved, pragmatic Swede. But underneath these simplistic stereotypes lie some important and consistent dimensions on which national cultures can be measured. The definitive work in this area was done by Dutch professor Geert Hofstede, who surveyed about 60,000 of IBM's workforce in the 1970s.

Hofstede identified four underlying dimensions of national culture that were relevant at work.

- **Individualism–Collectivism** – The relationship between the individual and the collective in society. In high individualism countries everyone takes care of him or herself, and there is emphasis on individual initiative and achievement. In low individualism countries, people are born into extended families of clans, identity is based around the social system, and there is a strong belief in group decisions.
- **Power distance** – the level of inequality between individuals in society. High power distance countries typically have tall organisation pyramids, more centralisation of power, and large wage differentials. Low power distance countries have flatter, more decentralised organisations, and smaller wage differentials.
- **Uncertainty avoidance** – the ease with which individuals cope with the uncertainty about the future. High uncertainty avoidance countries exhibit emotional resistance to change, higher job stress and less risk-taking. People prefer to work in large, stable organisations that create order and structure. Low uncertainty avoidance countries exhibit greater openness to change, and more risk-taking. People are comfortable working in smaller, more entrepreneurial organisations, and with relatively few rules.

- **Masculinity–Femininity** – the extent to which people (of both genders) exhibit typical masculine or feminine qualities. In high masculinity countries people are more assertive, more work-focused, and more concerned about recognition for their contribution. In low masculinity countries people are more nurturing, more concerned about relationships and the quality of their work environment, and they see work as less central in their lives.

The scores for Sweden, the UK, and a number of other countries are shown below. All scores are between 0 and 100.

Individualism	Power distance	Uncertainty avoidance	Masculinity
USA 91	Philippines 94	Japan 92	Japan 95
UK 89	France 68	France 86	Italy 70
Italy 76	Italy 50	Italy 75	UK 66
Sweden 71	USA 40	Germany 65	Germany 66
France 70	Germany 35	USA 46	USA 62
Germany 67	UK 35	UK 35	France 43
Japan 46	Sweden 31	Sweden 29	Sweden 5
Venezuela 12	Austria 11	Singapore 8	

Source: Geert Hofstede, *Culture's Consequences*, Sage (1980).

Notes

1 See Geert Hofstede, *Culture's Consequences*, Sage (1980); Fons Trompenaars and Charles Hampden-Turner, *Riding the Waves of Culture* (1998).
2 Author interview.
3 Author interview.
4 www.londonbusinessforum.com, 11 December 2001.

LEADERS DO THE SVEN THING 3

'Now they are writing a lot of good things, but if we lose it will, of course, be the opposite. So that is why as a football player or a manager, you have to try to be in the middle, always. Always think you are never as good as they tell you when you beat Germany 5–1 away, and you are never as bad as they tell you when you lose. You are some place in the middle.'

– Sven-Göran Eriksson

The new leadership

e argue that there is a distinctive Swedish style of leadership. Does it work? Well, think of this. 'Can't pass, can't keep possession, can't carry out instructions and give the ball away too much,' reflected Kevin Keegan of the England team after they had been knocked out of the European championships by Romania in June 2000. He was right. England were awful. Yet, just over a year later the English team were able to pass, retain possession and carry out their instructions.

The English team which beat Germany 5–1 away from home in one of the most dramatic victories in English football history included the core of the team – Seaman, Neville, Beckham, Scholes, Owen and Barmby – which had surrendered lamely the previous autumn to Germany at Wembley.

If much of the team remains the same, the difference lies not in the make-up of the team but in the performance of the team and in the identity of the manager. Leadership, on and off the pitch, can make the difference between ignominy and victory.

This applies equally to the business world. Successful companies are, in the main, well led companies. This explains why leadership has been examined from every angle imaginable. A once-obscure academic subject has become a heavy industry with book after book, conference after conference, guru after guru.

Over the last decade we have seen a shift in emphasis. The leadership role models of the 1980s were action-oriented, charismatic visionaries – Jack Welch and Lee Iacocca in the US, James Hanson and John Harvey-Jones in the UK. The leadership gurus of that era argued that leaders distinguish themselves from managers by challenging the status quo. They set direction, they motivate people, and they lead by example.

In the 1990s a different school of thought about leadership began to emerge – one built on softer attributes such as listening skills, consensus and sensitivity. This school of thought has many interlocking strands:

- William Peace, a Westinghouse executive, wrote a highly influential article in the *Harvard Business Review* in 1991 with the opening line 'I am a soft manager.' He went on to describe how soft qualities, like openness, sensitivity, and acknowledgement of weaknesses, were central to his success as a leader of people.

- Daniel Goleman, best-selling author of *Emotional Intelligence* argues – not surprisingly – that emotional intelligence is the key ingredient in effective leadership. There are five components to emotional intelligence at work – self awareness, self-regulation, motivation, empathy, and social skill.

- Rob Goffee and Gareth Jones, two British writers, argue that good leaders have a high level of authenticity and self-awareness. Contrary to much of the received wisdom, they suggest that inspirational leaders selectively show their weaknesses, they rely a lot on intuition to shape their actions, they reveal what makes them different from their employees, and they show empathy.

- Jim Collins, an American consultant, identifies 'Level 5 leadership' as the key ingredient in business transformation. Level 5 leaders, he argues, build enduring greatness 'through a paradoxical combination of personal humility plus professional will'. These individuals are not the larger-than-life characters that Americans typically associate with leadership. Instead they are often shy, unpretentious and even awkward – people like Darwin Smith the CEO of Kimberly-Clark who when asked about his leadership style eventually came up with the word 'eccentric'.

Sven Atterhed of Swedish firm the ForeSight Group suggests that Collins's categorisation neatly fits Eriksson's leadership style. 'I believe that Eriksson shares many characteristics of the best of Swedish leaders. Even more so I think that he shares the characteristics of Level 5 leaders, as described by Jim Collins. Sven-Göran is a prototypical Level 5 leader as I understand it. He keeps a very low profile publicly and is very shy of publicity. He puts the team and the task ahead of himself. He is extremely conscientious in selection of team members. He engages the WHOLE team (including those on the bench) and he searches for the "brutal facts". Once he has made up his mind he is totally determined (but not ruthless). All of the above agrees with the particular leadership found among the companies studied by Collins. That leadership is basically completely opposite to what you read about in much of the business press, which usually feature the charismatic loudmouths with bold visions and many words, who usually have weak people around them.'[1]

The current emphasis on 'soft' leadership should not be over-played. At one level it is nothing more than a fad – an over-reaction to the emphasis placed on the more macho and charismatic aspects of leadership during the 1980s. As London Business School Professor Rob Goffee notes: 'The trouble with leadership is that academically speaking it is a weak field – there are few fundamental truths. And as such, it is susceptible to fads and fashions. At the moment, the emphasis is on emotional intelligence, self-awareness, and Level 5 leadership. But the pendulum will swing again.'[2]

While leadership is more prone to faddishness than other sub-jects, there is an underlying shift in thinking about leadership that plays into the hands of understated, modest leaders like Sven-Göran Eriksson. Back in the early days of leadership studies (in the 1920s) researchers tried to understand the personality traits that separated leaders from followers – with generally disappointing results. In the 1940s the focus shifted towards what leaders actually *do* – their style of leadership. But it quickly became clear that there were many effective styles – autocratic leadership can be highly effective, but so can demo-cratic leadership. So this led in more recent years to what academics call contingency theory – which means essentially that different styles are appropriate in different situations.

The conventional wisdom today is that there are many valid lead-ership models. You can be successful whatever your personal quali-ties and whatever your background. But – and this is the key – you have to recognise your own strengths and weaknesses. If your style is inherently motivational and relationship-based, then you had bet-ter make sure you have a number two who is good at the operational side of the business. Many companies today make this separation ex-plicit. The CEO is the outward-facing executive, concerned primarily with direction setting and relationships with customers and financial markets. Meanwhile, the COO is the inward-facing executive, good at implementation and operational control.

Self-awareness, in other words, is an overarching quality that helps leaders understand what their style is, and where they need additional support. And this is where the Sven-Göran Erikssons of this world have a built-in advantage. Think of a simple matrix with task orientation on the vertical axis, and relationship orientation on

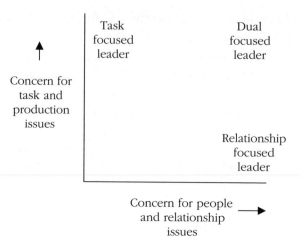

Task
focused
leader

Dual
focused
leader

Concern for
task and
production
issues

Relationship
focused
leader

Concern for people
and relationship
issues

the horizontal (above).[3] In reality most people are strong on one dimension or the other. Only about 13 per cent are actually strong on both (i.e. the top right 'dual focused leader' box). 'But the interesting insight from this framework', explains Rob Goffee, 'is that task-oriented people are apt to delude themselves – they are often convinced that they are also strong on the relationship dimension of leadership, when their employees know full well that is not the case. In contrast, the group who are strong on relationship management typically know full well that they are weaker on the task dimension. And they can compensate accordingly.'[4]

It looks like nice guys do actually finish first, after all. While the emphasis on self-awareness and empathy has some fashion-like qualities, there are also reasons to believe that this new model of leadership is here to stay.

So that's the theory. The trouble is that, in practice, business people can appear to remain locked in the past. A survey of human resource directors in the UK carried out by the Impact Development Training Group reveals that old habits die hard. The survey identified the five most important leadership traits as (in order of importance): drive; honesty; confidence; energy; and intelligence. The least important were: physical size or strength; aggressiveness; popularity; openness about feelings; and independence.

It is interesting that drive and energy feature so prominently. This suggests that sheer physical presence and stamina is still regarded as critical to leadership. Equally, characteristics at the touchy-feely end of the spectrum – such as openness about feelings – are not valued.

Insensitivity continues to rule – in our minds at least. Another element to this research is leadership role models. These are sadly predictable – Richard Branson (liked by women in particular), Churchill (the male choice) and Gandhi (the caring choice).

This is only part of the story, suggests leadership expert Phil Hodgson of the business school Ashridge. 'There are many organisations where the five leadership traits identified in the survey remain important,' says Hodgson. 'But as e-business, biotechnology and new organisational shapes prove themselves other leadership styles are emerging. Traits such as independence and openness about feelings may become more important as will the ability to handle ambiguity and uncertainty. New role models – such as John Chambers of Cisco and Amazon's Jeff Bezos – are also emerging.'[5]

David Williams, managing director of Impact, believes a new generation of leaders with different values and aspirations is now coming through. 'Truly inspirational leadership comes from within, from tapping into who we really are and combining that with skills and knowledge.' Impact has developed a leadership programme called 'Heroes' – a dangerous title in these politically correct times – which, according to Williams, 'gives participants the opportunity to explore who they really are, increase self-awareness and use what they find in a positive way.'[6]

The message is that, like it or not, the boundaries of leadership really are moving. Internally, leadership is becoming more personal. Individual leadership styles are now more prominent than leadership templates. Discovering the leader within – rather than someone else's take on the subject – is the new order of the day. Philip Slater, an American academic-turned-writer argues that 'Leadership is as much craft as science. Like the physician, it is important for the leader to follow the maxim "know thyself" so that he can control some of the pernicious effects he may create unwittingly.'[7] And listen to the emergent agenda set by the American leadership theorist Warren Bennis: 'I want to understand human development. I think that's the new challenge. In the future we will see chairs in cognitive psychology and human development established in schools of business.'[8] The heavy industry of leadership has, indeed, gone soft around the edges.

Eriksson: the new leader

Sven-Göran Eriksson is in many ways the archetypal new leader. He has soft skills, he is definitely not charismatic, but gets things done through people. He achieves results in different ways than the dictatorial leaders of yesteryear.

Three key attributes emerge from an analysis of Eriksson's leadership style – situation sensing (being aware of the situation and adapting accordingly), authenticity (being true to himself) and identifying with the team (seeing the world through their eyes).

First, situation sensing. 'Great leaders,' argues Rob Goffee, 'are very adept at sensing the atmosphere in their organisation. They can sniff out the signals in the environment and sense what's going on without having anything spelled out for them'.

Sven-Göran Eriksson exhibits this attribute very clearly. The players report that he seems to be floating around the edges. Tord Grip, Brian Kidd, Sammy Lee and others do most of the day-to-day coaching work. Eriksson spends most of his time observing – creating the ambience, and looking for the right opportunity to intervene. Eriksson also refrains from speaking too much – a sure sign of a relationship-oriented leader rather than a task-oriented leader. As Goffee observes: 'Task-oriented leaders love the sound of their own voice. Eriksson, like many others who are more focused on the relationship side, does a lot of looking and listening, and is comfortable with silence. Which has enormous benefits, because a lot of the information on atmosphere is non-verbal. It needs sensing.'

Good situation sensors don't just soak up the atmosphere – they also act on the signals they receive. Eriksson is in constant discussion with Grip and his other assistants, looking for ways to help them do their job better. And he is also skilled at taking players aside for low-key, one-to-one chats. At a conference in London, Eriksson was asked about how he handles the dressing room prior to a big match: 'I prefer not to give a pep talk to the team. It is very individual how players behave. Some don't want to talk to anyone. They want to make sure their shoes are tied, they want to sit by themselves. And if you play football, you can't expect 20 players to have the same manner in the dressing room. So I prefer a very quiet dressing room. But then I go round and talk with all of them, thirty seconds, one minute, two minutes with each – remember, let the ball go wider, and so on.'[9]

A second key attribute of great leaders is that they are true to themselves. They are authentic. This means accepting their limitations, and also knowing what sets them apart from others. From the followers' perspective this is a highly attractive feature, because it means a real person is leading them. Followers want to be able to relate to their leaders – to realise that they have anxieties and weaknesses, just like everyone else.

Authenticity is not something that can be measured, but it can be quickly sensed. As Rob Goffee puts it: 'We are all born with a built-in bullshitometer. We can tell pretty quickly when someone is bullshitting – when they are not being authentic. And we don't put up with it for long.' Sincerity can never be faked.

How does authenticity manifest itself? Great leaders, Goffee argues, will often reveal certain weaknesses (though, of course, not weaknesses that detract from actually doing their job). In Sven-Göran Eriksson's case, a clear weakness is language. His English is, of course, excellent but it is not perfect – and certainly he speaks it less well than he does Swedish and Italian. Given the media interest in his role, Eriksson might have tried to limit the number of press conferences he gave, he might have hid behind an interpreter, or he might have secretly invested all his spare time in sharpening up his English. But he chose to do none of these things. Instead he gives plenty of press conferences, and as a result his utterances often end up coming across as simplistic or stilted. 'This is who I am' he is saying, 'just like anyone else who moves to a foreign country, I struggle with the language'.

The Chelsea coach Claudio Ranieri has taken a similar approach. Initially he used an interpreter. Soon, however, he was giving press conferences in his limited English. This played a major part in overturning initial suspicion of his appointment to replace the popular Gianlucca Vialli and his often confusing tactics. When he speaks, Ranieri is playful. He delights in his use and mis-use of language. But what is clear is that he knows a great deal about the game and is very passionate about succeeding. He comes across as a fan.

The point is that while language errors reveal Eriksson – and Ranieri – as a 'real person', they do not detract from his ability to do his job. Compare this to the weaknesses his predecessors revealed. Kevin Keegan flagged his lack of coaching experience even while he was being pursued by the Football Association for the job, and then on the night he resigned he essentially told the press he was not up to the job. And Glenn Hoddle got into trouble talking about his religious beliefs – nothing to do with the job as such, but close enough to ruin his credibility as a national media figure. He resigned soon afterwards.

But while Eriksson is prepared to show others that he is like them in many ways, he is also definitively different at the same time. The stereotypical British football manager is a gung-ho, excitable, rather colourful personality, typically an ex-player, and not necessarily the brightest. Eriksson, in contrast, comes across as calm, thoughtful, intelligent, and urbane. He is Swedish, speaks four languages, and is a true cosmopolitan. He does not fit the classic profile. He is different. But that is also an authentic part of his make-up.

The third key attribute of great leaders is empathy – the ability to identify with their team, and see the world through their eyes. Again, this makes a leader someone people want to rally around – the leader understands what the team members are going through, and has probably been there.

In the world of football, identifying with the team usually comes from having been a player. In fact, football in the UK is unusual in the extent to which having been a player – even if not necessarily a good one – is a key qualification for the job. Interestingly, this is not entirely the case overseas. In Italy, for example, coaching qualifications are more important than a playing record. As a result, a star player like David Platt could not officially become a club coach because he didn't have the requisite qualifications. (Of course, being Italy, there is always a way around this rule.) This is the equivalent of insisting that every CEO has an MBA.

But identifying with the players is not enough, because if the leader focuses on how similar he is to his team, then the team will start questioning why he is the boss. Kevin Keegan fell into this trap – he got on famously well with the team, staying up late playing cards. But he was less good at distancing himself when tough decisions had to be made.

So leaders do not just identify with their team – they differentiate themselves as well. And this is the real trick. The leader has to know when to get close, when to empathise with a struggling player. And he has to know when to stand back, and take a more authoritative position. It is a paradox, and the ability to resolve it is a sign of a world class leader. As Rob Goffee observes: 'Knowing when to be close with your players, and when to pull back, takes world-class situation sensing. And Eriksson seems to do this really well.'[10]

Think back to the controversy surrounding Rio Ferdinand's non-attendance at a drug test prior to the crucial match against Turkey in 2003. The England team talked of strike action. Eriksson was pilloried for sitting on the fence between the team and his cmployers, the FA. Critics said that he didn't give a lead and was overly diplomatic. But Eriksson was right. He realised that if threw his weight behind the team he would have antagonised his employer and vice versa. Diplomacy was the right approach – and not necessarily the easiest one. Fences are uncomfortable places to sit.

Because most football managers come up through the playing ranks, they often have trouble with creating distance between them and their players. It's easy to be 'one of the boys' and all that entails – such as tolerating beer-drinking or staying out late. But it's harder to pull back, and as a result many managers end up falling back on what we can call the autocratic bastard mode. And good managers need a lot more range to their management style than that. Manchester United's Sir Alex Ferguson clearly does. He plays the autocrat very well, but he can also be charming, disingenuous, protective of his players, and a number of other styles in between. Sven-Göran Eriksson is in a slightly unusual position, because he is already different. He displays empathy in his one-to-one chats with the players, but he is by default somewhat removed from the world his team revolves in.

Old leaders	New leaders
Charismatic	Understated
Action oriented	Reflective
Idealistic	Pragmatic
Top-down	Bottom-up
Motivate through fear and intimidation	Motivate through reason and inspiration
Task focus	Relationship focus
IQ	Emotional intelligence
Self confidence	Self awareness
Jack Welch, Winston Churchill, Rupert Murdoch	Richard Branson, Sven-Göran Eriksson

Swedish leadership

The survey mentioned earlier showed that human resource directors in the UK still emphasise drive, energy and charisma as attributes of leadership. But the story in Sweden is very different. Researchers have highlighted the importance of teamwork and cooperation, the ability to create consensus and commitment around a vision, and a preference for direct dialogue with team members. As two Swedish academics, Edstrom and Jonsson, state: 'Swedish leadership is vague and imprecise. The typical Swedish order, see what you can do about it, has to do with a far-reaching delegation of authority. It indicates trust for co-workers, and it is also about executing control by a common understanding of the problem, rather than direct orders.'[11]

Ingalil Holmberg and Staffan Åkerblom, two other Swedish academics, studied the attributes of outstanding leaders based on articles in Swedish newspapers and magazines. These were:

- Performance and action oriented
- Charismatic and visible within and outside the organisation
- Honest
- Modest
- Pragmatic
- A good team-builder
- Work for egalitarianism and consensus
- Entrepreneurial
- Procedural.

The first two are familiar, but terms like modest, pragmatic, and egalitarianism are a world apart from the qualities of the archetypal British or American leader. But they are clearly relevant in Sweden.

Consider Ingvar Kamprad, the founder and owner of IKEA. Kamprad's leadership was highly unorthodox. He emphasised an informal business environment, an absence of status and conventions, and a highly egalitarian management style – all very Swedish. But he was also obsessed with detail. As one executive noted: 'He checks everything. He does not seem to believe in delegation, he is constantly bypassing formal structures to talk directly with front-line managers'.

Kamprad was also well known for cost control – 'there is no first class travel in IKEA,' he said.[12] Kamprad famously still catches buses.

Percy Barnevik, the former chief executive of ABB, is another interesting case. He is softly spoken, thoughtful, and pragmatic. He is good at pulling people together, and he loathes indecision. But he is less typically Swedish in other ways – he likes the spotlight, he can be terse and impatient, and he shows little balance between home and work life ('I am in the office two days a week, he once remarked, "Saturday and Sunday").[13]

But while Kamprad and Barnevik exhibit many of the key traits of Swedish leadership, their colourful personalities are highly atypical. The more typical examples Swedish leadership are the chief executives who shy away from the limelight – Leif Johansson at Volvo, Carl-Henric Svanberg at Ericsson, Lars Petterson at Sandvik.

Leadership in the sports world

Eriksson is evidence that a similar evolution has been happening in the world of sports leadership as has happened in business leadership.

Of course, the role of leadership in creating successful and sports teams has long been recognised. The second half of the twentieth century saw the rise of sports management as a distinct discipline.

Prior to the 1950s, football managers were important but tended to be marginal. They organised training and picked the team, but little else. There was limited consideration of tactics or the well being of the players. The media clamour was minimal. In the next fifty years their role changed beyond recognition. Managers strode in from the fringe. Their personalities shaped entire clubs and national sides – think of Rinus Michels with Holland; Bill Shankly at Liverpool; Sir Matt Busby at Manchester United.

Their leadership template was clear and uncomplicated. They ruled by edict and led through unstinting belief in a set of core values (usually involving hard work and taking football seriously).

Some football managers remain locked in the leadership dark ages. They rule through fear rather than persuasion; they are intimidatory rather than subtle. Thankfully for players the numbers of such managers are dwindling fast.

The rise of the mass media has now elevated sports coaches and managers to superstar status. They command large salaries and are engaged in a perpetual merry go round, moving from job to job. But that does not mean that football managers have well honed modern leadership skills.

Some unquestionably do. Manchester United coach Sir Alex Ferguson had a reputation as an old fashioned disciplinarian. He threw cups across the dressing room, he shouted and exhorted. Over the years, Ferguson's approach has changed. He hasn't lost his passion, but has discovered some degree of subtlety – remarks that annoy the opposition, a soft hand as well as a hard disciplinarian fist. When Paul Scholes failed to turn up for a match in late 2001, Ferguson was a model of understanding and restraint. He knew that the last thing that the sensitive and out-of-form Scholes needed was a fiery Scottish reprimand ringing in his ears. Scholes returned to form soon after. (The downside for Scholes is that Ferguson has a long memory for such things.)

The emerging generation of soccer managers and coaches are in the new leadership mould. In the UK think of the Arsenal coach Arsene Wenger, an urbane, (usually) mild mannered Frenchman; the Celtic coach, Martin O'Neill, who resembles a hyperactive sociology lecturer; or Aston Villa's David O'Leary, a softly spoken Irishman who has seemingly mastered the art of diplomatic fatuousness. All of these leaders offer a more sophisticated, people-centred approach to leadership. But, at the same time, they also seem to know when to impose themselves.

Sporting leadership and coaching have become more open minded. Sports teams embrace psychologists, dieticians, hypnotists and faith healers. John Beck, former manager of the English football club Cambridge United, has talked about his management style as developing from commanding to guiding. Perhaps more interestingly he used to leave notes in the changing room to inspire his players – not your average notes but quotations from Hippocrates and other words of wisdom from the philosophical greats. On Beck's departure, a radio report commented: 'His unusual approach to management – which Beck himself has described as both scientific and psychological – has included use of motivational posters, cold showers and even allegedly head-butting Claridge [a player].

Beck has also been criticised for gamesmanship such as under-inflating opponents' balls for the pre-match warm-up.'

And the rise of the new leadership model is not restricted to football. The World Cup-winning England rugby team is managed by former player Sir Clive Woodward, but most of the day-to-day coaching is devolved to his 16-strong squad of coaches and assistant-coaches. Andy Robinson, one of the team observes: 'There is no hierarchy and I like that. We all feed off each other and recognise that we are there for the players and not for each other's ego. There is an open discussion as to the game plan for a particular match.'[14]

Leadership by Sven

Many of the principles of leadership have been well established for decades. Good leaders are judged by their ability to attract followers, and by the results they achieve. Leadership is more art than science. Leaders are made not born. There are many different styles of leadership, and each has its place.

But the practice of leadership is evolving as well, and if we stand back far enough we can identify some broad changes. Changes in the qualities we look for in our leaders. And changes in the role models we look up to.

Sven-Göran Eriksson is by no means unique in his leadership style, but he offers us a visible and successful example of this new model of leadership. And so, what are the characteristics of leadership the Sven-Göran Eriksson way? It is multi-faceted. There is no single thing you can point to as the core of his leadership style. Leadership is complex and Eriksson is a complex character. In the chapters that follow, we pull out the different elements which, we believe, form the essence of his leadership style:

- Leaders are Different
- The Leader as Coach
- Keep Your Distance
- Motivate to Win
- There is an I in Team
- Keep it Simple
- Never Walk Alone
- Open Goals
- Face Up to Failure.

Notes

1 Author interview.
2 Author interview.
3 This matrix was first proposed in Robert Blake and Jane Mouton, *The Managerial Grid*, Advanced Management Office Executive, 1962, 1(9).
4 Author interview.
5 Author interview.
6 Author interview.
7 Philip Slater, Leading Yourself, in W. Bennis, G. Spreitzer, T. Cummings, *The Future of Leadership*, Jossey Bass, 2001.
8 Author interview.
9 Interview with George Yip, 28 September 2001.
10 Author interview.
11 A. Edstrom and J. Jonsson, Svenskt Ledarskap, in B. Czarniawska, *Organisationsteori pa Svenska*. Liber Ekonomi, Malmo.
12 Taken from Harvard Business School case study, 'Ingvar Kamprad and IKEA', 9-390-132.
13 Taken from Harvard Business School case study 'Asea Brown Boveri', 9-192-139.
14 *Daily Telegraph*, February 17 2001.

LEADERS ARE DIFFERENT 4

'You must never think you know everything about football.'

– Sven-Göran Eriksson[1]

Difference rules

The most obvious leadership lesson from Sven-Göran Eriksson is that you don't have to have been a great player to become a great coach. Leadership requires different skills. Leadership is different and leaders are different.

Central to Sven-Göran Eriksson's skills and mindset is an awareness that leadership requires a certain distance – we talk about this later – and that leadership is a unique professional role rather than a means of simply staying in football. From an early stage Eriksson has approached coaching in a rigorous professional way. Early on he visited clubs he admired, such as Liverpool, and took notes assiduously. He learned from the best and sought inspiration from as many sources as possible. He was, for example, an early proponent of sports psychology. For him coaching was as noble and necessary a calling as playing the game. 'I have always been very interested in sports psychology. I like to read, talk to people about that,' he has reflected.[2]

We make no claims that this is an amazing insight. It is not. But what is amazing is how many times it is completely overlooked. People are repeatedly put into leadership positions when they have limited leadership skills and limited leadership potential. They become leaders by default. Some surprise everyone and, against all expectations, develop leadership skills. Most do not. Leaders cannot be conjured from the air.

In the football world this is increasingly evident. Great players do not necessarily or automatically make the best coaches. There are exceptions – Kenny Dalglish at Liverpool, Johann Cruyff at Barcelona – but they are few in number.

The Dutchman Ruud Gullitt is a good example of this phenomenon. A wonderful player with AC Milan, Sampdoria and Holland, he became the coach of Chelsea and then of Newcastle United, purporting to offer 'sexy football'. This proved short-lived and largely sexless. Gullitt's man management skills were questioned. He fell out with star players – most famously with Alan Shearer who he eventually relegated to substitute. The suspicion is that Gullitt found the transition from being the centre of attention on the pitch to becoming responsible for the team too difficult.

Other players have similarly failed to make the transition to a leadership position. Gianlucca Vialli began his managerial career with a glass of champagne for his players, but was quickly tasting the indifferent spumante of failure with Watford. England star Chris Waddle tried his managerial hand briefly with Burnley and then swapped it for broadcasting. Liverpool player Mark Lawrenson followed a similar path after an unsuccessful stint in management.

Leadership requires an array of new skills. Look at what happened to Kevin Keegan, Eriksson's predecessor at England and now manager of Manchester City. Keegan found himself in a situation commonly encountered by managers. He was acknowledged by all and sundry as a master of motivation. The players admired him and enjoyed working with him. He was one of them. But his motivational skills were not matched by tactical awareness. As a result, under Keegan the highly motivated English team played soccer with the tactical awareness of headless chickens.

In business terms Keegan's problem was that he failed to make the leap from the nitty-gritty of making things happen to creating an awareness of the big picture. The English players are as skilled as any, but if they do not know what they should be doing and where they are going, they quickly become disoriented. They look to the coach for direction; a strategy to enable them to use their skills for the best of the team.

Generals and generalists

The same phenomenon plays itself out in the business world. Financial or legal specialists may not make the best CEOs. Bob Ayling, British Airways' former CEO, was the company's legal counsel before being promoted to the top job, and many felt that he lacked the people skills needed to be a great leader. Equally, a passionate interest in one particular aspect of marketing may be highly useful in one area of the business, but is not enough for the top job. Many companies now address this problem through carefully-managed career development programmes. High potential managers will be given opportunities in different functional areas and different businesses to round out their skill base.

Kevin Keegan's undeniable skills proved not to be those of the modern leader. This problem is commonly encountered in the business world – as the heavy churn of senior executives proves. Leadership experts Randall White and Phil Hodgson have mapped out the standard career progression. They suggest that there are three leaps in the development of senior managers. First, they become 'supervisors'. This tends to teach managers that there's more to success than just the technical aspects of the job and that, largely, people are a problem.

Then, at mid-levels in most people's careers, they are faced with the first leadership paradox. Suddenly, technical mastery of a given area isn't enough because the people who work for you will know more about a particular area than you. Learning to direct and motivate people who often do not want you to be their leader becomes a necessary skill. You also need to learn to be a creative problem-solver, sorting the strategic from the tactical and the urgent from the non-urgent.

The toughest transition is to become a generalist, a general manager – a process which Harvard Business School's John Kotter suggests takes a mammoth 20 years. 'At this level, the executive is supposed to be strategic and to be able to deal with the ambiguity inherent in the job. Here there are no right or wrong answers but only good, better and best answers,' say White and Hodgson. 'And so, the skills that propel executives up the ladder are not the leadership skills and perspectives needed for making it to the top. Higher order people skills, strategic skills and the skills necessary to deal with uncertainty are needed'. Jim Collins, author of *Good to Great*, thinks in terms of a hierarchy of skills. 'Level 5' leaders have all the qualities associated with the first four levels. But in addition they have an additional set of quite-different skills – a combination of personal humility and professional will (see box, Level 5 leadership).

The transition to general manager is an ongoing process of learning. As White and Hodgson observe: 'Not unimportant in this process is the notion that you are exposed to these skills every day – on the job. So the trick is to be open to learning on a daily basis. For individuals this involves taking risks and not being afraid of getting things wrong. For organisations this involves selecting individuals who are learners and making the most of the experiences available for learning.'

This progression emphasises the simple point that leaders are very different from managers. As John Kotter argues: 'Management

Level 5 leadership

The journey from capable individual to manager to leader is a long one, and it involves the development of multiple new skills at each stage along the way. Jim Collins, author of *Good to Great*, argues that there are five levels in the hierarchy of skills.

- Level 1 – Highly capable individual. Makes productive contributions through talent, knowledge, skills and good work habits.
- Level 2 – Contributing team member. Contributions to the achievement of the group; works effectively with others.
- Level 3 – Organises people and resources toward pursuit of predetermined objectives.
- Level 4 – Catalyses commitment to and pursuit of a clear and compelling vision; stimulates high performance.
- Level 5 – Builds enduring greatness through combination of personal humility and professional will.

Source: Jim Collins, *Good to Great*, 2001.

is all about coping with complexity, leadership is about coping with change.'[3] So managers cope with complexity through such activities as planning and budgeting, organising, controlling and problem-solving. Leaders, at the same time, are more concerned with setting direction, motivating and inspiring people. The two roles are very different, but they are also entirely complementary.

So, despite being a great communicator and motivator, Kevin Keegan failed to make the leap from specialist to generalist. However, there is a point of departure in comparing Keegan with your average CEO. The most notable fact is that he accurately identified his own shortcomings, decided they could not be solved and had the honesty to admit failure and walk away. There are few, if any, instances of executives following this route. The sad fact is that CEOs usually resign for poor financial performance and little else (see the box: Reasons for leaving).

Yet, the complex and pressured nature of managerial work means there must be many senior managers who find themselves in jobs they

Reasons for leaving: the habits of highly ineffective CEOs

In 2000, *Fortune* magazine conducted a survey of American CEOs who were forced out of their job during the 1990s. They identified four primary reasons:

- Bad earnings news – the most common problem, though usually seen in combination with some of the other causes.
- People problems – failure to get on with other senior executives, with the board, or with the owners.
- Lifer syndrome – too long in the job, lack of new ideas, part of the problem.
- Decision gridlock – lots of good ideas, but lacking in political clout to get them implemented.

The most damning statistic of all was the short tenure of many of the CEOs who were kicked out. Gil Amelio lasted one year at Apple, Al Dunlap lasted two years at Sunbeam, and William Fields lasted just one year at Blockbuster, then two at Hudson Bay.

Source: *Fortune* magazine.

are not equipped to do or jobs they simply do not enjoy. This partly explains the rise in coaching and counselling for senior executives. Kevin Keegan may well have benefited from such an arrangement. But, would people think any the less of CEOs if they raised their hands and admitted they were in the wrong job?

Developing leaders

The logical conclusion from all of this is that successful leaders are developed over time rather than thrust into leadership roles. The second conclusion is that leaders tend to have a persuasive grounding in reality. They may be visionaries, but while their head is in the clouds their feet are firmly on the ground.

First, let's look at what organisations need to do if they are to develop the leaders of tomorrow.

- **Understand the skills required.** Complex global markets require more sophisticated management skills, including international sensitivity, cultural fluency, technological literacy, and, most critically, leadership. Much the same rules apply to football: more sophisticated times demand more sophisticated leadership skills.

- **Think of teams of leaders.** Renaissance men and women are rare. 'Leadership in a modern organisation is highly complex, and it is increasingly difficult – sometimes impossible – to find all the necessary traits in a single person,' says Jonas Ridderstråle of the Stockholm School of Economics and co-author of *Funky Business*. 'In the future, we will see leadership groups rather than individual leaders.'[4] As well as ear-marking individuals, development needs to focus on groups of potential leaders with sympathetic skills. Leadership is a matter of team work (as our later section on teamworking emphasises).

- **Seek out role models.** Eriksson sought out his role models in the teams he admired. Liverpool, for example, were a long-term inspiration to him. Their management philosophy was based on developing leaders from within. Their most successful coach was Bob Paisley, whose quiet homespun approach to the game and the job has clear echoes with that of Eriksson. In business, as in football, role models of global leaders are few in number. Developing leaders is highly problematical in an environment in which the role models are limited in number. Seek and you shall find.

- **Provide experience.** People need to be stretched and challenged. 'There is one linking feature among those who become CEOs,' says David Norburn of London's Imperial College. 'Between the ages of 25 and 35 they have been stretched beyond the norm through things like job rotations, international assignments, functional rotation. They have been treated as mini-CEOs. This requires commitment from senior managers and a degree of selflessness and protectiveness not usually seen.' Look at the way Eriksson was stretched early in his career at Gothenburg and the way in which he encourages others to take on broader responsibilities and new roles.

- **Provide international experience.** 'Global leaders require a global cultural perspective. Without a global mindset, there are no global managers,' says Jonas Ridderstråle. 'Sending people out on international assignments early on in their career is crucial. Part of developing global leaders is a question of changing attitudes in subsidiaries so that they are given more responsibility. This requires leaders who understand what goes on – culturally and commercially – at that level. Global experience breeds global role models.'[5] As we shall see, at the heart of Swedish leadership is an unmatched appetite for internationalism.

- **Recruit lovers of uncertainty.** 'Companies need to search for people who deal well with uncertainty, ambiguity and change,' advises leadership expert Randall White. 'They should be wary of people who believe in one right answer to problems. Instead, they must seek out people who are able to adjust their thinking to fit a variety of situations. They must find people with cultural sensitivity – people able to eat peas with chopsticks, as someone once put it. Global leaders do things differently in a variety of locations, situations and culture and make it work.'[6] The willingness to be flexible and adaptable is key to leadership – no matter which sphere leadership is being practiced.

- **Plan for the future.** Developing leaders is not about the here and now. Look at the long-term development plans which lie at the heart of France's success in building a World Cup winning team and creating a coaching system and dynasty. Eriksson is charged with a similar job in England. Yes, results on the pitch are the ultimate arbiter of success, but that must mean results in the long-term. Another measure of success is whether Eriksson can build a coaching system which survives when he leaves. The same principles apply to organisations. 'Organisations will need to grow their own talent if they are to definitively address the leadership dilemma,' says William C. Byham, president and CEO of Development Dimensions International. 'At the same time, they are courting failure if they think they can simply dust off traditional success planning initiatives or refill standard talent pools. These are anaemic alternatives, at best. A far better strategy is developing an acceleration pool made up of leadership candidates from a range of different leadership levels. Given sufficient resources and attention, an acceleration pool provides the leverage to both respond to the immediate talent gap and grow outstanding talent for the future.'[7]

- **Love context.** Leadership is highly context specific. Leading England provides different challenges than managing Lazio. People in organisations need to think deliberately and perpetually about the strange nature of the linkages that connect everything they do. Leadership requires not only the exercise of direction in organisations it requires the understanding of the contexts in which the action must be exercised.
- **Start young.** Nokia chief Jorma Jaakko Ollila had an education which was a little more unorthodox than most, but which started honing his leadership skills early on in life. Aged 17, he was recommended for a scholarship at Atlantic College by his school headmaster. Atlantic College, situated in Wales, in the UK, is a unique educational establishment founded by Kurt Hahn in 1962, a German national, who evolved a distinctive educational philosophy. The rationale behind the college is to bring together individuals with leadership qualities who then go on to become political or commercial leaders throughout the world. Ollila was part of the school's first intake.

Leaders have dirty hands

A commitment to developing leaders is one aspect of recognising that leaders really are different. The second part of this is that leaders are grounded. Eriksson is grounded in reality thanks to his humble background and his indifferent playing career. Again this might appear easy – after all, his background had nothing to do with Eriksson – but is much harder than it seems. As the plaudits and money flow in, it is human nature for many to forget their grounding. The best leaders do not.

Think of IKEA founder Ingvar Kamprad. Born in the barren county of Småland in Sweden, Kamprad grew up during the Great Depression of the 1920s. He took the qualities of resourcefulness he saw around him to heart. The thrifty, hard-working ideals of his Swedish homeland were applied them to the retail business. Starting with matches he moved onto furniture and ended up with one of the largest furniture retailers in the world. Now in his seventies, he refers to the values he instilled in IKEA as the 'testament of a furniture dealer'.

It is summed up in a mission statement: 'To contribute to a better everyday working life for the majority of people, by offering a wide range of home furnishing items of good design and function, at prices so low that the majority of people can afford to buy them.'

It's a home-spun philosophy which combines the virtues of simplicity and making do, with a commitment to equality and innovation. It's an approach in step with today's times. The company was one of the first to use recycled materials in furniture, for example, more out of a desire to keep costs down than to be seen as green.

Building on its early experience in Sweden – when a visit to an IKEA store could involve a day's travel – the company has developed a distinctively integrated approach to retailing which aims to make shopping an enjoyable experience rather than a chore.

Cynics may question whether its folksy, for the people, philosophy can truly survive the transition to a big business, but the IKEA employees are genuinely committed to it. According to one senior IKEA executive at the company's headquarters in the Swedish town of Almhult: 'The only way of keeping the customer long-term in our vision is that he has a benefit from coming to IKEA. The product and price quality that we offer must be the best. We even say that we must have better prices than our competitors as one of our operating principles. That is basic to our long-term success.

'From there we say how can we make a visit to IKEA a day out. IKEA should be a day out. That started in the first store here in Almhult. In the old days to come to our store they had to leave early in the morning. The journey would usually take a couple of hours and many of our customers had small children.'[8] Hence the family restaurants and crèche facilities that have become a feature of IKEA stores (on weekends and holidays, the company even employs clowns and magicians to entertain the kids).

The logic is pragmatic. 'We believe that the prices in our restaurants should be very good so that customers with young families can afford to eat there and not have to bring sandwiches. They shouldn't have to leave IKEA just because they are hungry.'

The same sort of egalitarian principles apply to the management culture. IKEA permits no status symbols and refers to all employees as co-workers. The philosophy is reinforced by the example of Anders

Moberg, the company's most recent president, who was hand-picked by Kamprad. When travelling on business, for example, Moberg is famous for flying economy class, and refuses to take taxis when public transport is available. True to its small company roots, too, IKEA carries out relatively little customer research into new products, relying instead on a feel for the market.

The message from Kamprad is that leadership is about simple principles, keeping in touch with where you come from.

If you look at the great soccer managers it is notable that a large number were far from great players. The other notable thing is that many retained a strong grounding in the real world of work as opposed to the more glamorous world of playing football in front of packed crowds. Their origins are often humble – like Eriksson's.

The Manchester United manager Sir Alex Ferguson retired at 32 after an indifferent playing career in Scotland only worthy of mention because of a short period with Rangers. He then went on to run a pub in Glasgow before being lured into management. Running a pub in Glasgow provides preparation for virtually any job in the world.

Sven yourself

- When did your leadership training begin?
- What skills do you think are required of leaders in your organisation?
- Which of these skills do you already have?
- Which do you not possess?
- What are you doing about acquiring your missing skills?
- Is your organisation creating teams of leaders?
- Who are your leadership role models?
- What have you learned from them?
- What early career experiences have shaped your thinking and behaviour?
- Have you ever worked in other countries?
- How do you respond to uncertainty?
- Would you seek out uncertainty?
- Do you make long-term decisions about your development or does your employer?

Similarly, the legendary Celtic manager Jock Stein worked in coal mines until he was 27. His playing career was unexceptional. The hugely successful Liverpool manager Bob Paisley was a member of the club's backroom staff for many years. He, too, had a far from glittering career.

In Europe look at the career of Helenio Herrera the coach of Barcelona and Internazionale in the 1960s. Herrera was raised in the slums of Casablanca and became a naturalised Frenchman during his unexceptional playing career. (He, too, was a full back.) Herrera became highly successful as a coach and, in his heyday in the late 1960s, was reputedly earning the then massive sum, of £50,000 a year.

Leadership is different, but it appears that this is more likely to be appreciated by leaders who have a clear idea of what matters in life, the realities of working life, and where they come.

Notes

1 Interview with George Yip, 28 September 2001.
2 Interview with George Yip, 28 September 2001.
3 Kotter, John, 'What leaders really do', *Harvard Business Review*, 1990.
4 Author interview.
5 Author interview.
6 Author interview.
7 Author interview.
8 Crainer, Stuart and Dearlove, Des, *The Ultimate Book of Brands,* Capstone, 1999.

THE LEADER AS 5 COACH

'Whether it's sports or business, winning and losing doesn't depend on trick plays or new systems. It comes down to motivating people to work hard and prepare to play as a team that really counts. In a word, it's coaching.'

– American football coach Don Shula

It's one on one

At the heart of Sven-Göran Eriksson's management style is the one-on-one relationships he builds with the members of the England squad. 'He's good at man-management, group management and tactics. He is quiet, but not aloof and can be subtly inspirational. He is a definite winner,' says the former England player David Platt now coach of the England Under-21 team.[1] Eriksson connects with people. He doesn't need to make a barnstorming speech. Just a few words. A minute. A personal connection is better than a lengthy speech that nobody listens to.

Eriksson's one-on-one management style can be boiled down to two elements – empowering and coaching. Empowering is about delegating responsibility to the people who work for you, sharing decision making with them, and appreciating their initiative. Coaching is about making everyone feel part of the team, encouraging players to cooperate, keeping them informed and taking an interest in their individual performance.

The trouble with empowering and coaching as key elements of a management philosophy is that both terms are overworked to the point of cliché. Management theories including the human relations school of the 1930s and the socio-technical movement of the 1950s have emphasised the importance of empowerment and coaching as ways of getting the most out of your employees. It is a rare manager who will openly admit to doing the opposite – to restricting his employees access to information, or ignoring their ideas.

But the reality is that most managers neither empower their employees nor do they coach them. Some think they do, even if their employees know otherwise. And others implicitly adopt a rather different style. It is worth exploring this paradox in some detail.

The definitive research on this subject is the doctoral thesis work of Lena Zander, an academic at the Stockholm School of Economics.[2] She looked at the way managers relate to their subordinates (by asking the subordinates) in 18 different countries. After analysing the questionnaire returns of some 17,000 people, she was able to show that the one-on-one relationships bosses develop with their subordinates differ significantly from country to country. So, for example, in Britain people tend to see coaching as an important aspect of the boss's style, whereas for Germans it is more or less irrelevant.

At the heart of Zander's analysis were three different models:[3]

Anglo-American management

British and American employees emphasise empowering and coaching. This helps to explain the clichéd use of these terms, because it is typically management gurus from these two countries who emphasise them, often in the mistaken belief that they represent a universal style of management. For example Tom Peters, the American management guru, enthuses about the coaching style of leadership: 'Coaching is face-to-face leadership that pulls people together from diverse backgrounds, encourages them to step up to responsibility and continued achievement, and treats them as full scale partners. It is about really paying attention to people, really believing them, really involving them.'[4]

But there is an inherent conflict in this style – empowering is about giving employees the space and the skills to do things for themselves, coaching is about taking a personal interest in employees, encouraging them, and generally getting involved in their day-to-day activities. And it is often difficult to get the balance right. Think about your own working environment. When the boss comes over to ask you how things are going, is he coaching and motivating you, or is he checking up on you? The answer is probably a bit of both, but this means that empowerment is getting compromised for the sake of coaching.

And coaching also has problems of its own. While the term was picked up by the world of business from the world of sport, it is applied in a variety of ways. For some, coaching is about providing the supporting skills and ideas to help the individual excel. To others it is just about setting appropriate targets. To others it has a negative connotation. One colleague of ours was told that she would get some 'coaching' from the chief executive, which turned out to be a critique of her work. When coaching can mean so many things, it is little wonder that it gets in the way of true empowerment.

How not to empower your employees

- Regard any new idea from below with suspicion.
- Ask departments to challenge each other's proposals.
- Treat problems as a sign of failure.
- Insist people who need your approval go through several other levels of management first.
- Make sure any request for information is fully justified.
- Above all, remember that you, the higher-ups, know everything important about this business.

Source: Rosabeth Moss Kanter, *The Change Masters*, 1986.

Swedish management

Swedes (as well as other Scandinavians) emphasise empowerment, but they are less keen on coaching, and they dislike close supervision intensely. In other words they favour a model that gives them a lot of freedom to do their work uninterrupted by their boss. They believe they should be given a particular objective to meet, but it should be up to them to figure out *how* to meet it. And they think the boss should be prepared to take *their* advice on matters concerning their area of responsibility.

This is a very grown-up style of management. For the boss, it requires complete trust in his or her subordinates – a sense that they have the skills they need to carry out their job, and a belief that they have the maturity to act in the interests of the company or the team when faced with difficult decisions. Listen to Glenn Hysén who played under Eriksson at Gothenburg and Fiorentina: 'He's not much of a tactician. He doesn't spend a long time discussing what to do. He trusts the players.'[5]

A similar level of trust was evident in the relationship between Sir Clive Woodward and the England World Cup winning rugby team. During the break before extra time in the World Cup Final, Woodward did not have to give a highly charged motivational speech because his senior players were already saying exactly what he would have said. Trust and understanding were mutual. The boss even has to accept that sometimes the wrong decisions will be made, or that work will not be done as well as it might be, because some learning only happens through mistakes. Örjan Sölvell, the Director of the Institute of International Business in Stockholm told us that he prefers not to give his employees individual budgets. 'I want people to make smart decisions for themselves,' he explained. 'It is up to them to figure out how much to spend. Some money is wasted, but eventually they learn what is best for themselves, and for the rest of us.' By keeping everyone informed about the financial state of the institute, he reasoned that his team of researchers would act responsibly.

German management

Germans have a very different image of the boss-subordinate relationship than their British, American and Swedish counterparts. The boss, in their view, should focus less on empowering, and should downplay coaching altogether. Instead, they believe that they should receive frequent supervision and reviews of their work from their boss. They also don't believe that their bosses should take an interest in their personal lives.

These elements are consistent with most people's crude stereotype of German management – the rigid hierarchy, the careful attention to detail, the impersonal nature of the workplace. It also squares with the simplistic generalisations made about the all-too-frequent defeats the England football team has met at the hands of the Germans – where British creativity and flair has yielded to Germanic efficiency and order. But remember that this is not idle speculation – it is careful social science research and these ratings are simply a summary of how Germans assess their own preferences. It is also worth remembering that this model – despite its impersonal, machine-like form – also applies broadly to a number of other countries, including France, Switzerland and Japan. A group of countries, by the way, whose economic performance over the last twenty years has been at least as good as Britain's or America's.

Empowerment and coaching, in other words, are not universally desirable attributes. Lena Zander's research shows that in the UK and America both are seen as positive, but in many countries there are other ways of working that are equally effective. And of course these are not just national traits – there will be differences between companies in the same country, and differences between managers in the same company. Try rating your own preferred style using the questionnaire below.

What is your preferred management style?

For each of the questions, rate our answer on a scale where 1 = completely disagree, 3 = neutral, 5 = completely agree. Add up your total scores for Empowering and Coaching, and plot them on the graph below.

Empowering

1	The boss should delegate responsibility to his employees	1	2	3	4	5
2	The boss should avoid reviewing the employees' work too frequently	1	2	3	4	5
3	Decision-making should be shared between the boss and his employees	1	2	3	4	5
4	Employee initiative should be appreciated and welcomed by the boss	1	2	3	4	5
5	The boss should take advice from employees	1	2	3	4	5

Total

(*Continued overleaf.*)

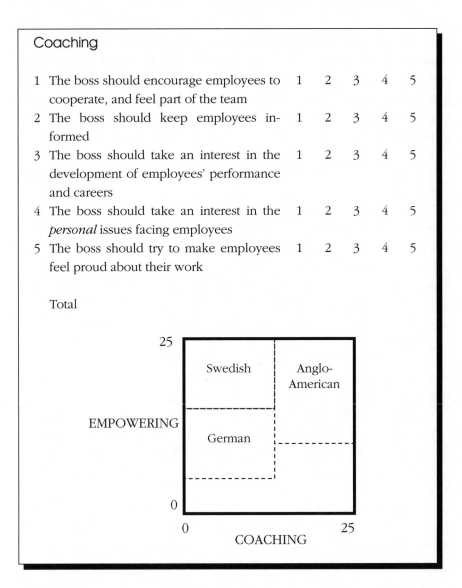

Coaching

1 The boss should encourage employees to   1   2   3   4   5
   cooperate, and feel part of the team
2 The boss should keep employees in-   1   2   3   4   5
   formed
3 The boss should take an interest in the   1   2   3   4   5
   development of employees' performance
   and careers
4 The boss should take an interest in the   1   2   3   4   5
   personal issues facing employees
5 The boss should try to make employees   1   2   3   4   5
   feel proud about their work

   Total

Adapting the Swedish model

While these different management models are all clearly valid, they are not 'pure' types. British companies can learn from the efficiency and order of the German and Japanese models. And they can also learn from the Swedish model. The problem with the Anglo-American model, as described earlier, is that the typical boss-subordinate relationship ends up being stuck in the middle. The employee is not given the level of close supervision that he might get in a German company. And he is not given the freedom he might get in a Swedish company. Instead, the boss understands the logic of empowerment – the need to give her subordinates responsibility for their own actions. But she has also learnt about the importance of 'coaching' her team – spending time with them, developing them, and taking an interest in their personal life. In trying to balance the two, she ends up getting neither right. And employees become confused by the mixed messages they are receiving.

The Swedish model, in contrast, is internally consistent. It is essentially about letting go. It applies equally to relationships at home, at work, and on the football pitch. And it is exemplified by Sven-Göran Eriksson. He does not meddle in the details that his assistants and his players can figure out better for themselves. He keeps his distance. But he also spends time with each player, identifying challenges and problems they are facing, and looking for ways to motivate and develop them.

Of course the Swedish model has its own built-in tensions. You need to give people the space to make their own decisions, but you also have to define clear boundaries beyond which they should not roam. You need to give them the power to act, but if you give them too much power without the necessary skills and training, they can make expensive mistakes. But if you can get the necessary balance in these areas, it is a very powerful model because it frees up the creativity and talent of your entire workforce.

So if this is such an attractive model, why is it so rare elsewhere? There are a couple of reasons. First, it should be seen as a Swedish model because it is in keeping with some of the underlying cultural traits of the Swedish people. Swedes, as mentioned in chapter 2, are very good at coping with uncertainty. And they are not obsessed with hierarchical position. These factors make it much easier for the boss to let his subordinate take full responsibility for an area of the business. In contrast, the pure empowerment model is anathema to the traditional British manager who equates his elevated position in the hierarchy with power and with superior knowledge. (This is reflected in the FA's selection of managers. Its selection policy was always – until the arrival of Eriksson – built around finding someone with superior knowledge to manage in a superior sort of way.)

Applying the Swedish model in a traditional British company is like pushing a rock up a hill – you can do it if you push hard enough, but one false step and the rock will roll back and crush you.

Think of some British business leaders of the last twenty years – James Hanson of the eponymous conglomerate; Arnold Weinstock of General Electric; or Sir Richard Greenbury of Marks & Spencer. They ruled their companies with an iron fist – they used a combination of detailed knowledge of their businesses with careful and systematic control systems, and they generated strong loyalty from those managers who appreciated their command-and-control style. As Lord Hanson remarked: 'I believe very firmly in the combination of carrot and stick. We make it crystal clear what the manager's task is, but don't just leave it to him or allow him to get on with it. We require him to do it. This has a dramatic effect on the individual. Possibly for the first time in his career, he senses the meaning of responsibility.' Hanson (the company) grew rapidly on the back of this model, but it worked best when it was buying and splitting up undervalued conglomerates, or when trying to squeeze greater profitability out of badly-managed businesses.

But there is also an emerging style of management in the UK that looks a lot more like the Swedish model. Think of the Virgin group, which is now in a plethora of different businesses from airlines to financial services to coke. Virgin has been called a branded venture capitalist. Sir Richard Branson encourages employees to experiment with any number of new business ideas, which he provides seed money for. The company is flat, fast-moving, and entrepreneurial. Many ideas don't work out, but a few – like Virgin Atlantic – more than make up for the failures. Another example is British Petroleum (BP), a rare example of a large, lumbering giant of a company that has radically transformed itself from within. At the heart of BP's transformation is a style of management that places responsibility for delivering results deep down in the organisation. 'Contracts' are set between the top executives, Sir John Browne and those running BP's business units, and then those individuals are given free rein to deliver on their contract in whatever way they see fit. Call it empowerment, or call it entrepreneurship, the essence of the model is that success comes from a high level of commitment to an agreed objective. And the real beauty of it is that BP was once a bastion of traditional British management, with its deep hierarchy, and lifetime job security. Even a leopard, it seems, can change its spots if the rewards are great enough.

The second reason why the Swedish-style empowerment model is so difficult to pull off is that it is inherently fragile. When everything is going well it is easy for the manager to give his employees more slack, and to let them make mistakes. But as soon as problems emerge the knee-jerk reaction is to pull control back to the centre. We have seen this happen countless times in an international setting. Picture the following scenario. The subsidiary manager runs into a problem with a major local customer, and needs to spend all his time sorting it out. But his boss demands that he flies back to HQ to update him on the situation, and then insists on weekly updates thereafter. Of course, the boss at HQ can't solve the problem, but he craves the security of at least being kept updated on what the problem is, and how soon it will be fixed. In doing this, he actually makes it *more* difficult for the subsidiary manager to solve the problem. And even worse, a by-product of this little episode is that the subsidiary manager no longer feels empowered. It is fair-weather empowerment only, and that is not the same thing at all.

Theatre offers another example of the power of empowerment. Philip Slater, an American academic who became a novelist and playwright, observes that inexperienced playwrights often want to direct their own plays.[6] They are worried that others will not understand their vision, so they try to control the entire process. 'The result', he explains, 'is usually sterile and often disastrous. If the playwright's vision comes through in the writing, the director will see creative ways of enhancing that vision – ways that the playwright never dreamed of. And so will the actors, designers, composers, and so on.'

Slater's advice to playwriting students is *not* to set stage directions in detail, because they limit the actors' options. Good actors, he argues, have dozens of ways of creating a desired effect – ways the playwright probably has not thought of – and will choose the one that is most natural or appropriate to the context. The analogy is a powerful one – leaders, like playwrights, create a vision and provide a text for people to follow. But once that is done, they should stand back and let their people interpret and deliver on the vision. Too much micro-management limits people's opportunity to add value and take ownership of their piece of work.

How to coach the Sven-Göran Eriksson way

- Give employees targets and goals, not precise instructions.
- Ask employees their opinions on important issues.
- Give employees space – resist the temptation to interfere too often.
- Don't provide all the answers to employees' questions – help them to come up with their own solutions.
- Delegate any task that an employee can do 70 per cent as well as you can.
- Keep employees informed of changes in business, strategy, and financial position.
- Use praise more than criticism.
- Encourage initiative and a reasonable level of risk-taking.
- Reward well-intentioned failure.

Empowerment and coaching are universal concepts. They apply in the office, on the football pitch, on the stage, in the classroom, and in the home. So, the next major leadership lesson from Sven-Göran Eriksson is very simple: let go.

Leaders on the pitch

In the business world true examples of empowerment are the exception rather than the rule. One of the most glorious exceptions is the Brazilian company Semco. When Ricardo Semler took over this family business in 1980 it was unexceptional in performance and management. Given two to three weeks to change things, Semler set about restructuring it in a dramatic and revolutionary fashion. In a single day he fired 60 per cent of the company's top management. He based his revolution on three values: employee participation, profit sharing and open information systems. Semco now has just four grades of staff. The job of chief executive is handled by six senior managers for six months at a time (Semler is one of them). Managers set their own salaries and bonuses and are evaluated by those who work for them. Employees decide their own working hours, set quotas and improve products and processes. 'The company is organised – well, maybe that's not quite the right word for us – not to depend too much on any individual, especially me,' says Semler. 'I take it as a point of pride that twice on my return from long trips my office had been moved – and each time it got smaller. My role is that of a catalyst. I try to create an environment in which others make decisions. Success means not making them myself.'[7]

In the sporting world being able to empower people is vital to the leader's role. People must be allowed to get on with the job. The leader is left to sit and fret powerlessly on the sidelines.

Little wonder then that great teams have great captains. The proof of a sporting coach's ability to empower lies in the power invested in their captains, their leaders on the pitch. Football history suggests that great teams virtually always have well chosen leaders on the pitch. Think of a few.

- **Laurent Blanc, France** – as a player Blanc was slow and appeared unkempt with his socks falling down and unruly hair. But, as a captain, he proved inspirational. Blanc's gift was to exude Eriksson-like calmness at all times.
- **Bobby Moore, England** – defensive calmness personified. Moore was an early choice by Sir Alf Ramsey as England captain because he exuded leadership qualities.
- **Daniel Passarella, Argentina** – Passarella lifted the 1978 World Cup and was the rugged on-pitch manifestation of the chain smoking Argentinian coach Menotti.
- **Carlos Alberto, Brazil** – there were better players in the classic Brazil team of 1970 (Pele being one of them), but Carlos Alberto was the captain, a role he justified.
- **Franz Beckenbauer, Germany** – the Kaiser of cool combined elegance with defensive intelligence.
- **Michel Platini, France** – leadership as style. Sometimes it works when the best player rather than the best leader is made captain.
- **Franco Baresi, Milan** – the Milanese maestro; rarely pretty but always efficient.
- **Ruud Krol, Ajax and Holland** – in a superlative team, Krol was the undisputed captain – or as undisputed as the argumentative Dutch were ever likely to have.

What sort of qualities does the team captain have? First and foremost, he should lead by example. He has to be a player the others look up to – a world-class performer, probably highly experienced. Steve Jobs, CEO of Apple Computer argues that this model applies in the business world as well. 'We went through the stage at Apple when we thought, we are going to be a "big" company, lets hire professional managers. And it did not work. Most of them were bozos. I mean, they could manage, but they couldn't *do* anything. Do you know who the great managers really are? They are the great individual contributors – the ones who never wanted to be the manager, but they took the job because they realised they had to for the sake of the team.'[8]

Steve Jobs, in other words, picks his team captains by identifying the best players and giving them the extra responsibility. And Sven-Göran Eriksson operates with a similar philosophy. David Beckham got the nod, and his performance ever since has been exemplary. 'David Beckham has been just magnificent, an inspired choice as captain,' said former FA chief executive Adam Crozier. 'Beckham has grown into it in a way that even his biggest fans would not have imagined. The players have a fantastic amount of respect for him. He is so keen on the job and really works hard, talking to us, the players and the coaching staff. He's been a brilliant ambassador, and he has played out of his skin. If you put all that together, you couldn't ask for more from an England captain.'[9]

The team captain needs other qualities as well. He has to be in sync with the head coach's management style. He essentially represents the coach on the pitch, so it is important that he gives the players a consistent message. This approach was exemplified by England captain Bobby Moore who proved a hugely successful adjunct to Sir Alf Ramsey.

The captain must also be able to see the whole picture. This explains why, in football, captains are usually defenders who are better able to see the whole game. Forwards have an indifferent track record as captains. (This is particularly true in England's case where Gary Lineker and Alan Shearer were largely unsuccessful captains while being great players.)

In addition, the captain has to be able to think on his feet, and adapt to the competitive situation as it unfolds. We examine this point – particularly as it applies in a military context – in a later chapter.

Sven yourself

- Are you empowered? By whom?
- How do you empower other people?
- How do you coach people?
- How many people pass on their bright ideas to you?
- Who's your captain?

Notes

1 Anthony, Andrew, 'Svengland', *The Observer,* 5 August 2001.
2 Zander, Lena, *The Licence to Lead*, Institute of International Business, Stockholm, 1998.
3 There were other models as well, but typically exhibited by a much smaller number of countries, and with less distinctive characteristics.
4 Peters, Tom, and Austin, Nancy, *A Passion for Excellence*, HarperCollins, 1985.
5 Anthony, Andrew, 'Svengland', *The Observer,* 5 August 2001.
6 Slater, Philip, 'Leading yourself', in W. Bennis, G. Spreitzer and T. Cummings, *The Future of Leadership,* Jossey Bass, 2001.
7 Author interview.
8 Steve Jobs quoted in *In Search of Excellence* video, Tom Peters and Robert H. Waterman.
9 Campbell, Denis, 'The history man', *The Observer,* 13 January 2002.

KEEP YOUR DISTANCE 6

'English managers of the national team, including myself, really wanted to do it for the country. I'm not saying Sven doesn't want to do it, but there is an advantage for him in not being English. We carry with us the fact that we're representing our own country – the jingoism that is associated with the national team, the feeling that you've just got to do it. Not having that may be an advantage.'

– Graham Taylor,
former England coach[1]

Embracing the new

I t's easy to talk about the need to be open to new ideas, but hard to do. We are all, to some degree, captives of our past. We develop rules of thumb, opinions, beliefs, and prejudices, and we then apply them subconsciously whenever new challenges come along.

Why did Apple, the Californian company that first popularised the personal computer, so resolutely fail to adapt to the changing nature of the industry in the 1990s? They had access to the same information as everyone else, but Steve Jobs, John Sculley and the other Apple executives had become so obsessed with Apple as 'the only thing standing between IBM and industry domination' that they refused to accept the emergence of the Microsoft and Intel dominated PC world.

A leader needs a number of key attributes to be open to new ideas. As we've seen, he needs a strong number two who is prepared to speak his mind, as Eriksson has in Tord Grip. He needs a wealth of experience – from working in different countries, and working with different types of people. One of the distinctive things about Eriksson is his international pedigree. Coaching in Sweden, Portugal, and Italy before coming to England gave him a broad diversity of experiences to draw on. In contrast to a coach who has spent his whole career in England, Eriksson is unlikely to be blindsided by the latest tactics to emerge in the continental game.

The leader also needs a fair dose of humility – the sense of perspective and self-belief that allows him to challenge beliefs that he previously held to be true. Again, Eriksson's modest, self-effacing style is an asset here. He seems genuinely surprised at the media's interest in his every word, and he would as soon solicit the interviewer's opinion as answer his question.

So how can you develop an openness to ideas?

Well, first of all you need to beware of xenophobia – the fear of strangers – which is a common trait in countries but it is also widely seen in organisations of all sorts. Companies prefer to hire executives with a strong background in the industry, preferably from a blue-chip competitor. They benchmark aggressively against their peers. They incorporate features from their competitor's products in their own. And gradually, the leading players in the industry all look exactly like each other. What differentiates KPMG from Deloitte and Touche and the other members of the big four accounting firms? Not much. Can you *really* distinguish the products and services of Barclays Bank from those offered by Lloyds, HSBC, HBOS, and The Royal Bank of Scotland/NatWest? Probably not.

It is easy to see why companies copy one another. Conformity is safe. If a novel strategy goes wrong, the creator of that strategy can be personally held to blame. But if a me-too strategy goes wrong, then everyone is in the same boat, and the blame can be attributed to external factors. A study was done of North American banks lending money to Latin American countries in the 1980s, and the enormous write-offs they all ended up making. Not one executive lost his job as a result of these write-offs, essentially because all the banks had made similar levels of investment in the countries that defaulted. How can you fire someone for doing what was the standard industry practice?

The trouble is, copying competitors is guaranteed to lead to mediocrity – to very average levels of profitability. And then when the world changes, or a new customer need emerges, it is the complete outsider who capitalises on the opportunity. The examples of this are now standard business folklore – Starbucks in coffee, Amazon.com in books, Canon in copiers, Ryanair in airlines.

All of which underlines the risk the Football Association took in bringing in a foreign coach. The safe option would have been to pick from the usual gene pool – the English Premier League managers – even if there was little excitement about any of the candidates. But instead they plumped for an outsider, knowing very well that the press would have vilified them if things had not gone well.

Avoiding the xenophobia of past generations of business leaders is not easy. The track record of truly innovative companies like Virgin is mixed at best – there is still only one Richard Branson. But there are still some things you can do to improve your chances.

- **Hire from outside.** Bringing in a Swede to coach the England football team was predictably unpopular. There were cries that he did not understand the English game, that he would not be able to relate to the players. But the reality was that he knew the game as well as anyone, and in addition he brought a fresh perspective. The same is true in business – when Richard Branson got into the airline industry, he turned his lack of industry experience to his advantage, and pushed concepts that British Airways would not have countenanced.

- **Develop a view on the future.** 'As an activist for change, you need a point of view', argues Gary Hamel, the American business guru. This includes what is changing in the world, the opportunities those changes make possible, and the business concepts that would profitability exploit those changes. And crucially, this does not mean sticking within the traditional industry boundaries. A top football coach has to follow what is happening in other countries in the world, but he should also keep up to date with developments in ice hockey and American football, to see if there are any ideas that might work in football. The idea of 'pinch hitting' in baseball, for example, found its way into cricket in the mid-nineties and was very successful for a time.

- **Challenge your mental models.** Everybody has mental models, which help them to simplify and process the information they receive, but which at the same time constrain them. Costas Markides, the Robert Bauman Professor of Strategy at London Business School, says that companies have to actively question their mental models 'to think actively about assumptions we make about our business and about our behaviour in that business'.[2] There are many ways of doing this – creating a 'positive' crisis by giving the company a new target to aim for, developing a questioning culture, creating measures of organisational 'health' and experimenting with new ideas.

- **Be aware of new sources of ideas.** The bright new ideas almost never come from the executives running the company. They are typically the ones most ingrained in the traditions of the company, and they have most to lose if things change dramatically. Instead, the new ideas come from the edges – from the front-line people dealing directly with customers, and from the foreign subsidiaries. If a company is serious about innovation and change, it has to develop a way of pulling in and acting on the ideas that are buried deep inside the organisation.

Listen to Eriksson: 'If I have a player like David Seaman – I don't know how many games he has played for Arsenal and England – of course they have an opinion, and if you don't listen you are stupid. And I have always disliked people who know everything about everything, they're boring after five minutes. So you listen, and then of course you have to decide. The formation, I decide what to do. But taking information from others is important.'[3]

The view from the inside

The view of the outsider is valuable. But that is not to say that the people within the organisation – the insiders – have nothing to offer. Part of the trick of being an effective outsider, as we have seen, is a willingness to tap into the unused potential of those already inside the organisation.

After all, many companies pride themselves on their internal promotion model. Every year they bring in a wave of fresh graduates, they train them up, push the high potentials forward, and groom them for senior executive positions. This model works in industry after industry, country after country. Richard Greenbury spent 46 years at Marks & Spencer, Niall Fitzgerald started at Unilever 36 years ago, Nick Scheele, the number two executive at Ford, began his career there in 1966. Jack Welch, America's most famous CEO who recently retired, spent his entire career in a single company.

Insiders have enormous benefits – they have extensive personal networks, they know the company inside out, and they are deeply loyal. Executives at Caterpillar, the American earth-moving equipment company, used to talk about having 'yellow blood in their veins' – a reference to the colour of all their products.

But every coin has two sides. Loyalty, in-depth knowledge and personal networks are assets when times are good. But when times are bad, or at least changing, those same assets turn into liabilities. Strong personal relationships make it harder to fire people. In-depth knowledge often equates to a lack of knowledge of what is going on in the rest of the world. And loyalty can make even the smartest executive blind (see the box: What monkeys can teach managers).

Kevin Keegan, for example, had a close bond with Alan Shearer who he had signed for Newcastle United. While others suggested that

Shearer was past his best, Keegan was steadfastly loyal. Loyalty is a noble thing, but not when it is misplaced.

Keegan had no sense that the leader needed to adopt a certain distance. He wanted to be in the melée. He stayed up playing cards and watching boxing with the squad. He was anxious – perhaps over anxious – to be one of the lads, part of the team. Eriksson has never played at a high level. He has no pretensions to being part of the team in the playing sense. Again unlike previous managers, he does not micro-manage, nor does he get too friendly with the players. He is there, but distant.

So it is no surprise that companies often turn to outsiders at a time of crisis. Lou Gerstner took over at IBM in 1993 after a career in McKinsey and American Express. In 2001, BT replaced lifer Iain Vallance with Christopher Bland, formerly chairman of the BBC. Ericsson recently replaced chairman Lars Ramqvist with Michael Treschow, the former CEO of Electrolux and Atlas Copco.

Outsiders have three key advantages over insiders in difficult times. First, they have the benefit of objectivity. They are not emotionally attached to businesses that should have been closed long ago. 'I come from outside so I have no favourite players and no favourite clubs,' said Eriksson at the start.[4] His message was that he was an outsider with no axe to grind, no agenda, no political connections, no history.

Second, they come with a new perspective. They ask the difficult questions – why do we sell to our distributors this way? And they don't accept the answer, 'that's how we have always done it'. Often they can take ideas or concepts from their background in a different industry and apply them in their new environment.

Finally, outsiders typically have more degrees of freedom than insiders. The smart outsider makes sure these are negotiated up front before taking the job. But on top of their official mandate, outsiders also benefit from a lack of implicit obligations to the other people they are working with.

The leadership lesson here is that it is often easier to bring about change as an outsider. Eriksson had a first-class track record, but he came to England as a complete outsider. As he commented at a conference in London in 2001, 'when I got the offer, I did not really know how good or bad the team was'. While the press immediately picked up on his lack of knowledge of England players as a liability, he turned

What monkeys can teach managers

There are some monkeys, and they live in a cage. Not a small cage, but a massive cage, filled with and trees and tyres and all sorts. There is one route up to the top of the cage where, hanging on a rope, is a bunch of bananas. When the monkeys first move into the cage, one of their number heads straight for the bananas. Monkeys do this. Just as he reaches them, however, the keepers outside the cage turn a power hose on him, and on all the monkeys in the cage.

When they have dried off and regained their composure, another monkey has a go, with the same result. Wet monkeys. Eventually, after several goes at this, the monkeys get the message and go about their business without daring to make another break for the bananas.

A new monkey is introduced to the cage. He doesn't know what happens when you make a move for the bananas. So the new monkey heads up towards the top of the cage. But before he gets close to the bananas his new neighbours, fearful of another drenching, attack him ferociously. Battered and beaten, he doesn't make the same mistake again.

Gradually, all the original monkeys in the cage are replaced by new monkeys. On each monkey's introduction the same charade results. The monkey makes a move on the bananas, fellow monkeys bundle him before he gets there. Finally, even though none of the original monkeys who experienced the drenching remain, none of the monkeys make a move on the bananas. They're not really sure why. It's just the way things are done.

The moral: We often follow rules and policies blindly because we assume that they make sense and others know better than we do. But the logic behind these rules is often outdated. Think about this in your own workplace. Why do you do things this way? What if we tried something different?

Source: Matt Rowson, www.bsad.org

it into an asset. He and Tord Grip toured the country, they watched countless games, and they judged for themselves who should be in the team. Eriksson then made some tough decisions – pushing out

England stalwarts like Tony Adams and Martin Keown, and bringing in new blood. 'Some of the older players had been there a lifetime,' said Eriksson said. 'We took them away, and said, Ashley Cole, he is good, 19 years old. If he is the best left back in the country, let him play.'[5]

Media and madness

The challenge for leaders is to perform a balancing act. They must connect with people and yet must retain a distance. They must still be objective. They must see the bigger picture while still striking emotional chords with their followers. They must be outsiders and insiders at the same time. The trick is to retain the freshness of perspective which is the chief advantage of being an outsider with the ability to understand and utilise the networks and resources within the organisation.

At this Sven-Göran Eriksson is a master. Nowhere is Eriksson's ability to keep a distance better demonstrated than in his dealings with the media.

The British media is outlandish and excitable. 'The media thing and its pressures definitely puts managers off. People don't fancy it,' says Howard Wilkinson who was briefly England's caretaker manager.[6]

Since becoming English coach Eriksson has witnessed the full gamut of media excess. There have been pictures taken of him on vacation – the standard shots of the celebrity in swimming trunks, with female partner in an exotic location. There has been a song – 'The Sven song' by Bell and Durling which includes the memorable chorus: 'Sven Sven, Sven-Göran Eriksson/He's lovely geezer/(But don't forget he's from Sweden).' There was a full-page newspaper ad featuring a convincing spoof photograph of Eriksson in his underwear. He is wearing Union Jack underpants. He has also been compared to Montgomery Burns the nuclear power plant owner in *The Simpsons*. And then there was the excitable furore surrounding his relationship with Ulrika Johnson, remarkably the only other famous Swede resident in the UK.

Eriksson is unmoved by all this. He is gnomic, shoulder-shrugging and elusive. He plays the media game brilliantly. He gives so much of himself and then stops. 'I know there are people who don't want me here, and I am sorry for them. But if people have an opinion about me, I try not to respond,' is how he reacted to criticism of his appointment.[7]

During the 1994 World Cup in America, a Swedish television channel recruited Eriksson to offer some of his insights. When it comes to football, Eriksson is effusive and insightful – as you would expect. The televison company salivated at the prospect of bringing Sweden's brightest and most erudite young coach alongside the legendary commentator Arne Hegerfors. In conversation with Hegerfors, Eriksson was analytical perfection. Then the microphone was switched on. Eriksson's analytical style was transformed. Platitudes replaced insights. Instead of voicing opinions, Eriksson sat on the fence. Diplomacy ruled.

Eriksson is a natural diplomat. His relationship with the British press was a baptism of fire. They didn't want to like him. The mass market newspaper *The Sun*, reflected the mood circa September 2000 with its customary gusto: 'The nation which gave the game of football to the world has been forced to put a foreign coach in charge of its national team for the first time in its history. What a climb down. What a humiliation. What a terrible, pathetic, self-inflicted indictment. What an awful mess.'

Other newspapers fell in line with criticism of the appointment. 'England's humiliation knows no end. In their trendy eagerness to support a designer foreigner did [the FA] pause for so long as a moment to consider the depth of this insult to our national pride. We sell our birthright down the fjord to a nation of seven million skiers and hammer throwers who spend half their year living in total darkness.'

Eriksson showed incredible coolness in dealing with their questioning, saying as little as possible, avoiding the foot-in-mouth problem that many executives suffer from (as well as some of Eriksson's predecessors). Before the England-Sweden friendly in late 2001, Eriksson was asked about the national anthems of the two countries that would be played immediately prior to kick-off. 'Which anthem will I sing? Well, let's say I am a good listener.' With brilliant diplomacy Eriksson deflated the issue. When the time came, the cameras focused in on Eriksson who stood, as he promised, listening intently.

Faced with out and out prejudice, Eriksson responded with good natured understanding. 'I can understand the people are saying England should have an English manager,' he observed before mentioning George Raynor who guided Sweden to the World Cup final.[8]

His response to the media frenzy was to make sure he was seen in the right places (i.e. watching matches), keeping his statements short and simple to allow people to draw their own conclusions. He is akin to the Chauncey Gardener character in the Peter Sellers film *Being There*. Gardener is a naïve gardener whose gnomic utterances are interpreted as incredible profundities by a world anxious to believe. While Gardener was suggested as a possible President of America, Eriksson coach of England.

When silence is golden

And the lessons from Eriksson's diplomatic reluctance to sign over his life to the media? Silence really is golden. Most people seem to hate silence. Some see it is as a sign of inadequacy – that they have nothing to say. Some just love the sound of their own voice. Others find it embarrassing. But it turns out this is a highly culture-specific thing. In Britain or America the norm is for discussion to proceed essentially without gaps – with one speaker often cutting off the previous speaker. In Scandinavia and some Asian countries, in contrast, there are often significant gaps between speakers in a discussion. One of us attended a conference at which a well-known Japanese business-man was speaking. Every question to him was followed by a lengthy silence and then a carefully-worded, thoughtful response. For him, silence was simply thinking time but, for the mostly British audience, it was all horribly awkward.

Sven-Göran Eriksson makes good use of silence. When he is being interviewed he keeps his answers short, and he often pauses be-tween sentences. And in his coaching work, he keeps his discussions with the players short. Partly this is a cultural thing – silence is more acceptable in Sweden than in the UK. And the Finns are famously taciturn. Lena Zander, a business professor at the Stockholm School of Economics, used the term 'silent coaching' to refer to the Finns' preference for a boss who communicates infrequently and through non-verbal means.

But silence is also an interesting attribute of leadership in its own right. When used cleverly, it has a number of benefits:

- Silence gives others space to have their say. Good leaders, as discussed earlier, empathise and identify with their followers. And to do that effectively, they have to be good listeners. But listening is an art. If the leader asks her team what they think of her idea, she is likely to get the answer her team thinks she wants to hear. Real feedback – negative as well as positive – is much harder to get. And silence is a useful tactic. 'Are you happy with the direction this project is heading?' the leader may ask, and the team replies 'yes, absolutely'. But rather than moving on, the leader then pauses. After five seconds of painful silence, one team member steps in, 'well, I wonder if we need to revisit the delivery schedule …' Soon, a number of other issues have also surfaced.

- Silence accentuates what is said. Sven-Göran Eriksson is known as a man of few words. So when he speaks, people listen carefully. This is a very effective way of communicating. And very different from the archetypal politician who is able to talk endlessly without making a single point. People know bullshit when they hear it. And they quickly tune out. It is actually very difficult for someone who talks too much to get their point across, because the listener cannot distinguish the salient from the inconsequential. Eriksson even delegates many of the pre-match pep-talks to his assistants. This is part of his keep-your-distance style, but also part of his desire to speak only when he has something really important to say.

- Silence improves non-verbal communication. It is also important to remember that speech is only one of many means of communicating. Good leaders are adept at sensing what is going on – through conversation, but also through body language, changes of behaviour, who is talking to whom, and so on. Eriksson may not speak much during training or a match, but he is not sleeping on the job either – he is watching and listening, picking up non-verbal signals.

Notes

1 Draper, Ron, 'How Sven plotted quiet revolution', www.soccernet.com

2 Markides, Costas, 'Strategic innovation', *Sloan Management Review*, 1997
3 Interview with George Yip, 28 September 2001.
4 Anthony, Andrew, 'Svengland', *The Observer*, 5 August 2001.
5 Interview with George Yip, 28 September 2001.
6 Woolnough, Brian, *Poisoned Chalice*, Ebury, 2000.
7 Anthony, Andrew, 'Svengland', *The Observer*, 5 August 2001.
8 "Up to the job", http://sportsillustrated.cnn.com, November 2 2000.

7
MOTIVATE TO WIN

'He is already very tough. He can speak with the big stars to make them understand his way of thinking. He is very good at that.'

– Sven-Ake Olsson, Eriksson's first club coach[1]

Switching on the lights

T|ry this. Take £10 and leave the office in search of your lunch. Try a few shops. At each examine the behaviour of the people serving you. Do they appear to be motivated? Is the service good? Spend the money at the one with the best service and fritter away the change in as many shops as possible keeping a close eye on how you are served.

Your search for good service and highly motivated people may take some time, according to motivational expert David Freemantle. Freemantle is author of *The Stimulus Factor* and sends out people on his training programmes as mystery shoppers armed with ten pound notes. 'There are so many books and so many theories but it is quite obvious that people are often simply not motivated. Go into stores and you will find demotivated people. Why are there so many theories and so many demotivated people?' asks Freemantle.[2]

He may well ask. Indeed, our understanding of motivation remains bewilderingly vague, an unlikely and unappetising hotch-potch of carrots and sticks. Companies tend to provide a healthy diet of carrots early in their lives before discovering the motivational simplicity of sticks.

The classic motivational research was carried out at Western Electric's Hawthorne plant in Cicero, Illinois between 1927 and 1932. The Hawthorne studies began with experiments in which the lighting in the factory was altered. The theory was that brighter light would raise morale and, as a result, increase productivity. Hawthorne workers were separated into two groups. In one group the lighting levels were increased: productivity increased. In the other group the lighting remained at its normal level: productivity increased.

The researchers concluded that they had missed something. This something was the relationships, attitudes, feelings, and perceptions of the people involved. The research revolved around selecting small groups of workers to be studied. This, not surprisingly, made them feel special. For the first time they actually felt that management was interested in them. The second effect was that the people felt like they belonged to a select team. They identified with their group.

The message from Hawthorne was simply that if you pay attention to people they will perform better. Unfortunately, this is something which companies and managers tend to repeatedly forget. This also applies to the football world. There are many stories of players being ostracised and ignored on a managerial whim. (The brilliantly but unpredictably talented David Ginola, for example, spent some of the last seasons of his footballing career languishing in Aston Villa's second team, unwanted by the team coach.)

To make matters worse, attention is often of the wrong type. Look at the modern call centre. 'The technology is quite insidious,' says Gerry Griffin, author of *The Power Game*. 'Managers can monitor in real time the productivity of individuals. It is mechanistic; old economy management with new economy techniques. The information imbalance gives managers leverage which they can abuse.'[3] Managers can monitor success ratios, identify periods of high efficiency and inefficiency. If you perform poorly on a Tuesday morning after your regular late night on Monday, they will know.

Often, companies substitute money for attention. They give someone a pay rise and expect them to perform happily and efficiently. One of the by-products of the new economy bubble was that ownership rather than salary was a driving force. 'If you give technical people 50 per cent of a business and no salaries they will do wonderful things,' an Internet entrepreneur told us.

Employee ownership is not just a new-economy phenomenon. Xansa, the IT services company formerly called FI Group, has actively promoted this concept since it was founded, and around 32 per cent of the company is now owned by current employees. Hilary Cropper, executive chairman says: 'The employee ownership has profoundly changed this place. It affects every decision I take. I feel that I am working for the employees, not that they are working for me.'[4] Philip Cook, company secretary, observes: 'There is a genuine buzz about the place when people's performance drives the share price up. People can see the link between their efforts and the market cap of the company.'[5]

But employee ownership is not just about financial gain – it is about having a stake in the company you work for, and a sense that you are contributing to a higher-order purpose.

'Motivation is not as simple as people believe. It is not to do with money,' says David Freemantle. 'Sir Richard Branson didn't mention money once when I interviewed him. It's the challenge, doing things differently, working to achieve something.'[6]

Sceptics may suggest that the motivations of a multi-millionaire are liable to be non-financial. However, studies of the new generation joining the workforce suggest that money is no longer the prime motivator. It is not that the young are unmoved by financial reward, but that they recognise there is more to life.

What is more likely to motivate is a 'cool' work environment and a strong sense of community. Wander into a new company and you are likely to find open work spaces and community spaces, deep sofas, and kitchens with fridges filled to overflowing with free fizzy drinks and snacks. The time that the employees have to spend at the dentists is offset by their improved productivity.

Once again, Sweden is a natural home for many of these ideas. 'Exploiting the last taboo means departing from the tradition that people are to be treated as just another factor of production – a human resource or an anonymous consumer,' say Jonas Ridderstråle and Kjell Nordström in *Funky Business*. 'People do not enjoy being treated as human resources or as a nameless and faceless customer x; they want to be seen and recognised as individuals. We have to tap the hidden treasures of the extended organisational tribe and its members. We have to start competing on the basis of feelings and fantasy – emotion and imagination.'[7]

Icon Medialab, a Swedish Internet consultancy, is typical of the new breed of company that recognises the needs of the new generation of employees. Established in 1996 in the early days of the dotcom boom, its founders set about to create a high energy, high performance culture by offering what they called the '3M's', money, meaning, and magic. Icon's focus on money led it to be one of the first Swedish companies to offer stock options to all employees and to use performance bonuses as a significant part of an employee's pay. To create meaning, Icon pursues market-leading companies as clients, uses multidisciplinary teams to deliver projects, and allows 20 per cent of employees' time to be spent on training and development. To create magic, the founders promote a fast-paced, flexible, flat and close-knit organisation culture, locate their offices in prime locations, and keep the media spotlight on the firm's achievements. Employees are encouraged to be creative, go beyond acceptable solutions and try ideas that are new and innovative.[8]

All the carrots in the world may not attract some people to join up. The motivation to actually join a company is distinctly lacking among many of the so-called 'net generation'. Bruce Tulgan, author of the influential *Managing Generation X* has now turned his attention to people born between 1978 and 1984, the new generation. 'They are like GenXers on fast forward with self-esteem. They are self-confident and optimistic, independent and goal-oriented, masters of the internet and personal computer. They are young adults who believe education is cool, integrity is admirable, and parents are primary role models. They're blunt. They're savvy – and they're contradictory,' says Tulgan.[9]

Unquestionably, this new motivational order provides managers with headaches, especially managers more inclined to reach for the dimmer switch than actually paying attention to people. After all, if people are self-motivated how do you motivate a team?

Bruce Tulgan believes commitment is a two-way street. The key to managing the net generation, he says, is to find out what they really, really want and use it to get results. 'Managers often complain: "This one wants Thursdays off." "That one wants her own office even though she's been here three weeks." "This one wants to bring his dog to work." And so on. But managers are wrong to complain. When you discover the wants and needs of an individual contributor, you've cracked the motivation issue.'

'There is increasing awareness of emotional and spiritual stimuli,' says David Freemantle. 'We are paying the penalty for scientific management, treating people like robots. Too much emphasis is on mechanistic and rational processes. Some organisations are still in the dark ages. They're dominated by rules and regulations. Only recently have we realised the importance of emotion and spirit.

'It is much more complicated than designing financial carrots. We all get into routines and ruts at home and at work so we need fresh stimulus. Successful organisations provide that. They energise people.' He points to companies such as Starbucks, Pret A Manger and Virgin as motivational exemplars.

These are companies which try to allow people to be themselves. This, of course, was anathema to the great corporate model of the twentieth-century. Workers at Henry Ford's car plant or members of IBM's salesforce were not encouraged to be themselves. Dutiful facelessness was the order of the day. No more.

Turning Sven on

All of these motivational issues find a focus in the world of international sport. First, let's look at Sven-Göran Eriksson's personal motivation.

When he was a player at Torsby one of Eriksson's incentives was a series of cheap driving lessons offered by one of his neighbours if the club won promotion. They did. Mild mannered and quiet he may be, but Eriksson is a driven man.

You have to be. Executive coach Robert 'Dusty' Staub has coached more than 10,000 executives in leadership development and personal mastery. We asked him why people take on the top jobs. 'They do it because it's the right thing to do,' said Staub. 'They're on a track. It's a question of ego and ambition. To become a CEO you need to be highly competitive, highly driven, and somewhat neurotic. When someone like that has an opportunity they can't say no.'[10]

Eriksson is highly competitive, highly driven. Of that there is no doubt. He talked of playing football in Italy when he was a boy and, when his playing career failed to get him to the promised land of Serie A, he coached his way to the best teams in Italy. For Eriksson, money is no longer an issue. He has houses in Italy, Portugal and now London. He has been very well paid for a number of years and his current salary is hardly peanuts – in excess of £1 million – but it's not the prime reason he accepted the job.

'I did not take this job for the money, nor for the weather. I took it because it's a big challenge,' Eriksson said when his appointment was announced.[11]

For the leader, the challenge is all. Leaders accept challenges and also recognise that surmounting challenges is the route to large financial rewards. Eriksson has done so throughout his career. First there was Gothenburg who he converted from average domestic performers into serious contenders on the European stage. Then in Italy it was challenge after challenge. Lazio, for example, hadn't won the *scudetto* for 26 years. In addition, they are universally loathed, the team people dislike for no rational reason. And then Eriksson found England, a country with ridiculously high expectations whose team hasn't won anything for over 30 years and a team associated with jingoism, xenophobia and hooligans.

The message is that leaders take on challenges to develop their own skills. They lead and learn and are rewarded and motivated to do so.

Sven the motivator

The other side of the motivational coin is how does Eriksson motivate people? We asked motivational guru David Freemantle what he saw as Eriksson's motivational approach:

'Eriksson comes across to me as a man who can command respect and can be trusted. I suspect he is immune to personality, celebrity and the hype that goes with it and therefore focuses on the task in hand (score goals and win). To do this he needs to treat the players in his team as human beings as opposed to celebrities. I sense that he does this well (handling each player as a human being as opposed to a famous person).

'He creates the respect and trust by believing in his players, in their capability for sheer hard work (in Beckham's case in the World Cup qualifying match against Greece) and for giving their best. I suspect furthermore that he is tolerant when they have their off-days (as many of the players did in that match).

'Another key motivational stimulus which relates to focus is challenge. I do believe that for people to excel and to achieve results people must have short-term challenges ("this is what we agree you seek to achieve in the next 90 minutes").

'A final factor is that he focuses on the strengths and potential of each player. He doesn't play people out of position (as Keegan did) and therefore allows them to exploit their natural abilities and play to their own strengths. To do this he gives them a lot of freedom (as opposed to restricting them to a tight regulated game plan).'[12]

Eriksson's motivational methods boil down to three things: being positive, trusting people and providing calm focus.

Being positive

Eriksson's first couple of months in charge of England showed the power of positive thinking. 'I don't think England have done so badly that they need to drastically change. You need to be positive. You need to believe you are strong, and we are strong,' Eriksson said on his appointment.[13]

At a conference in London, Eriksson reflected on those first couple of months. 'My first task was to make the squad come together and start talking about going to the World Cup 2002. And anyone who does not believe in that can go home at once because being negative, not believing that we have the possibility, "being last in the group," I don't like that. And this positive spirit really showed itself against Germany. All of us said, we won't come here to lose this game. We will take a chance and win it. There are many positive players in this team. And maybe I changed that.'[14]

The most impressive aspect of this turnaround is how quickly it was achieved. 'I really admire the speed with which he changed the situation,' observes Robin Peddlar, an associate fellow at Templeton College, Oxford. 'Most companies plot change programmes over a number of years, but Eriksson came into a group of people who had a low opinion of themselves, and turned their performance around instantly.'[15]

Trusting people

Trust is the bedrock of strong relationships. Research has shown that leaders who radiate trust will quickly bring out the best in their employees, while leaders who are control freaks will engender risk-averse and narrow-minded behaviour. Or as Laurie Morgan, marketing director of Noble House puts it, 'If you expect people to fail, you will never be disappointed.'

Eriksson identifies (with Tord Grip) young talent, works with them, and gives them confidence in their abilities. His approach – as we discussed earlier – is to give the players space and to let them make their own mistakes.

Providing calm focus

'I don't think I am famous for being upset, very seldom, but it happens of course. In football, as in my private life. I am rather calm. I have always been like this, all the teams I have coached,' says Eriksson.[16]

Eriksson radiates calm. In the hectic world of professional football, calm is a valuable commodity in its own right. But it also reinforces the trusting relationships he builds with his players. Eriksson's approach is not to bark orders from the touchline – it is to work through his strategy in consultation with the players. In his own words, 'If you have people who try to do a good job, first you have to explain to them so they understand what to do. Then once they understand they have to accept that it is the right way to do things, it is the right way to play 4–4-2. When they understand it and accept it, then you can start working together – we are agreed, we shall do this'.[17]

And this approach has quickly found favour with the players. 'He has instilled self-belief. He does all his talking beforehand. I think he feels that's enough. He's not one to leap off the bench shouting orders,' observes star midfield player Steven Gerrard.[18]

Managing talent

Managing talent is a large part of the football manager's job. But it is also an increasingly important part of any management role, whether you work in entertainment, investment banking, IT or biotechnology. Industry after industry is being held hostage to the 'superstar' effect – where the key individuals figure out how valuable they are to their team, and ratchet up their earnings until they are extracting as much value (in salary and bonus) as they are generating for their employer. Frank Quattrone, the legendary Wall Street investment banker, managed to negotiate a contract worth $250 million plus profit share for him and his team when he moved to Credit Suisse First Boston, on the basis of his previous successes with Deutsche Morgan Grenfell and Morgan Stanley. Luis Figo managed to get Real Madrid to part with $30 million when he joined them from Barcelona. These numbers are almost never justified in retrospect, but such is the draw of the superstar player that companies or football teams fall over each other in the rush to sign them. Mariah Carey, the pop diva, signed a $70 million deal with EMI for five albums, but then EMI backed out of the deal and gave her a large pay-off.

One person who knows both the glamorous world of the entertainment business and the business world is Simon Best. Currently CEO of Ardana, an Edinburgh-based biotechnology company, in his earlier years he managed Sheffield pop group The Human League who had number one hits on both sides of the Atlantic. For him, the parallels between the two worlds are strong. 'Pop stars are high talent and high maintenance people. They can be very stubborn. They change their mind frequently. And they do not respond to normal incentives and arguments. Top class scientists are similar – they are not in it for the money, they work because they want to. They could work anywhere in the world, so they need to be constantly stimulated to stick around.'[19]

How do you manage talent? Simon Best's approach is based around respect for the individual, building their trust, and not interfering too much. 'I spend my time trying to secure commitments, and somehow helping them to deliver on these commitments. Because if they don't like my style, they will stop listening to me.'[20]

When it comes to managing talent, Eriksson has had a lot of experience. In Italy club owners rather than coaches usually buy the players. This means that the coaches often end up with players they do not want or particularly like. They have to make the best of it. Talent comes first rather than their fit within the team or their personality.

All of Eriksson's experience has been brought to bear in managing England's star player, David Beckham.

Think of what it is like to be David Beckham. He is in his twenties. He plays for the most famous football club in the world. He is married to a pop star. Everywhere he goes in the football playing world he is recognised. The media cover his every appearance, his every gnomic utterance. His tattoos and hair cuts have been photographed from every conceivable angle.

Think of how you would manage David Beckham.

What motivates him? It isn't money. How could you get the best possible performance from him? What would you do?

When he was the England manager, Glenn Hoddle conspicuously failed to come to terms with Beckham (at a time when Beckham's celebrity status was yet to explode). After Beckham was ingloriously sent-off against Argentina in the 1998 World Cup he sat in the dressing room after the game apologising to his team mates for his aberration – a flicked kick at the Argentinian Diego Simeone. Hoddle ignored him. Only the England captain, Tony Adams offered the distraught young player consolation.

So how would you motivate David Beckham? David Freemantle suggests ten strategies:

1   Treat him like a human being, not like a celebrity.
2   Develop and demonstrate mutual respect and mutual trust.
3   Encourage him to focus on the task in hand (winning the match).
4   Believe in him and show that you believe in him (and his capacity for sheer hard work and giving his best).
5   Be tolerant when he makes mistakes or has an 'off' day.
6   Set him short-term challenges.
7   Allow him to use his natural strengths on the field.
8   Give him freedom (do not restrict him too much).
9   Aligned with freedom is responsibility. Give him responsibility (as he has done).
10 Help him to further develop his potential.

Another motivational guru, Richard Denny says: 'The only way that David Beckham can be motivated and managed effectively is through recognition. I am sure that at this stage the next goal for him to aim for is to become the best British football captain in history, he has a long way to go. Also to become the best football player in the world, he still hasn't achieved that. So, there are a number of areas that he can be motivated towards, but it is all to do with recognition.'[21]

Eriksson has pretty much followed the advice of the experts. First, he recognised Beckham's talent and made him captain of the team. This was not a universally welcomed decision as there were still questions about Beckham's maturity and ability to cope under pressure. Second, he conspicuously offers Beckham respect. Look at Eriksson in a press conference with his captain. He looks admiringly at Beckham. He knows that he is a great player and nothing else matters. 'I'm not worried as long as he's a good player. It's up to him how he cuts his hair,' says Eriksson.[22]

All the rest is hype.

Sven yourself

- How do you rate your motivational skills?
- What motivates you?
- How big a factor is money?
- Does your working environment motivate you?
- Do you have any ownership of your business?
- Do people who work with you trust you? Do you trust them?
- Is your approach generally positive?
- How do you accentuate the positive?
- How are talented people managed in your organisation?

Notes

1 'Hometown hero', http://sportsillustrated.cnn.com, November 4 2000.
2 Author interview.
3 Author interview.
4 Author interview.
5 Author interview.
6 Author interview.
7 Ridderstråle, Jonas, & Nordström, Kjell, *Funky Business*, FT.com 2000.
8 Author interview.
9 Author interview.
10 Author interview.
11 'Up to the job', http://sportsillustrated.cnn.com, November 2 2000.
12 Author interview.
13 'Up to the job', http://sportsillustrated.cnn.com, November 2 2000.
14 Author interview.
15 Author interview.

16 Interview with George Yip, 28 September 2001.
17 Interview with George Yip, 28 September 2001.
18 Draper, Ron, 'How Sven plotted quiet revolution', www.soccernet.com
19 Author interview.
20 Author interview.
21 Author interview.
22 Anthony, Andrew, 'Svengland', *The Observer*, 5 August 2001.

THERE IS AN I IN TEAM 8

'If you are afraid you can never perform well. You must have respect and if you can have that respect you build a good atmosphere in the group.'

– Sven-Göran Eriksson[1]

Teams at work

P ut yourself in the shoes of a hypothetical retired businessman with a £100 million fortune and a passion for football. You would like nothing more than to take the lacklustre local team you have been supporting for decades and turn them into league champions. So you buy the team. Now what?

Well, everyone knows that you need a top quality manager to motivate and coach the team. So you pay top dollar to lure a proven manager from another Premier League club. And then on his advice you start buying talent – disaffected players from rival teams, up-and-coming names from overseas, and so on – until you have what looks on paper like a team that should be challenging for the title. You leave the manager to get on with the job, and you wait, and you wait. Players are bought, players are sold, and when things go really badly you sack your manager and bring in another. And still the crowning glory of a championship victory eludes you.

Money can't buy you love, and it can't buy you a championship-winning football team. This is the central paradox facing Sven-Göran Eriksson, or for that matter the manager of any team. It does not matter how talented the individuals are who make up the team – it is the team, the collective unit, that ultimately has to perform. Some teams are greater than the sum of the parts. Many end up being less than the sum of their parts. As the old aphorism has it, a team of stars does not make a star team.

This is a lesson that gets played out week after week in the English Premier League. There are teams like Manchester United and Charlton Athletic that have carefully nurtured their own home-grown talent through youth academies and talent scouts. These clubs have managed to build a sense of loyalty and commitment in their players, and in their supporters, and this faith is rewarded with consistent results, year after year. Then there are the likes of Chelsea, Fulham, and Blackburn, clubs with impressive rosters of star players but with a high churn rate as players and managers alike go in and out of favour. This model can work for a time, as Blackburn's single league championship win, or Chelsea's victories show. But the bedrock of consistency is missing, and performances are typically erratic.

Chelsea under Roman Abramovich is a case in point. With spending in excess of £100 million, Abramovich has certainly assembled the necessary talent for a league-winning team, and he may even end the season with one of the trophies he craves. But if so, it will likely be a fragile success. A squad of high-profile stars put together quickly – and through frequently overpaying – can be taken apart as quickly as it is put together.

Sven-Göran Eriksson could easily fall into the Chelsea trap. After all, he is free to choose from the wealth of footballing talent that a country of 50 million or so people has to offer. After each game he could look at the individual performances of the eleven players in the team, drop the two or three who were the least effective, and replace them with the latest crop of talent. He could make sure, in that way, that the best individual players were always in the team. But instead he takes a much more measured view.

When Eriksson picks a player, that individual typically gets a good run. He is loyal to them in the same way as he expects loyalty from them. (For this reason, it is notable that players have often played for Eriksson at more than one club. Typically, the Croatian Sinisa Mihajlovic played under Eriksson at Sampdoria then followed him to Lazio.)

Look at how Eriksson managed the England forward Andy Cole. The Blackburn Rovers player Cole (formerly with Manchester United) has been much maligned in what is by any stretch of the imagination a highly successful career. He has won medals in abundance and, along the way, has scored at an exceptional rate of around a goal every two games. But Cole's international record is as poor as his performances have been. Statistics can lie, but when it comes to Cole they do not. And yet, Eriksson stuck by him – he continued to pick him for England's qualifying games, and he resolutely defended his decision to the press. Whether this was the right decision is purely a matter of opinion, but Eriksson was correct to give Andy Cole the time and opportunity to become a valuable part of the team.

The former FA chief executive Adam Crozier, among those instrumental in bring Eriksson to England, has reflected on what Eriksson has brought to the team and concludes that it is: 'Calmness; confidence that if you know what you're asked to do, it'll work out; a sureness, or definiteness, about what they're being asked to do; simplicity; and real team spirit, which you can see.'[2] Crozier cites the team's celebrations when Cole scored his first England goal against Albania as evidence of togetherness and comradeship.

The leading academic Richard Scase is an expert on Swedish management styles. 'Teams are the basis for individual success,' he says. 'Eriksson has made England a team rather than a collection of players who get together to play football. For Kevin Keegan, it was built around two or three key players. Swedish companies are managed on the basis of teams as the foundation for the development of individual skills. Importance is given to developing shared knowledge, which provides the basis for the allocation of work tasks, decision making and techniques of self-management. All of this requires low staff turnover and long-term employee commitment – something that Eriksson is clearly fostering.'[3]

Mutual loyalty is the key. Again it is a Scandinanvian thing. Among the CEOs we interviewed while writing this book was Katherine Hammer of the American company Evolutionary Technologies International. We weren't talking to her about Eriksson, but what she said struck a chord. Hammer has a PhD in linguistics rather than an MBA. We asked if this had helped her career. 'There is a link between linguistics and programming,' she told us. 'Both describe patterns of behaviour. I also have a love of Norse and Celtic literature and would argue that their historical model of leadership is better-suited to today's IT world than the command and control model. Their notion of leadership was based on mutual recognition of the dependence of the leader on his warriors. Loyalty was mutually defined. The leader was obligated to set a good example, to reward people who demonstrated loyalty and, conversely, the warrior was obligated to be loyal to the leader. The worst thing you could do was to betray your leader.'[4]

It's in the walls

Why is a good team so much more than the sum of its parts? Management theorists have been pondering this question for generations, at least since Chester Barnard's classic treatise *The Functions of the Executive* written in 1938. What it comes down to is that value gets built up over time in the relationships between people, and in the 'walls' of the organisation for which they work. Take relationships first. As two people work together they get to understand each other's strengths and weaknesses, they develop short-hand ways of communicating, and they start to make sense of what motivates or frustrates the other. They begin to rely on and trust one another – they develop social capital, in the words of the theorists. It is much easier for David Beckham and Paul Scholes to pull off a neat one-two when they have been playing together for a decade, than for two players who only get together six times a year for England.

Value also gets built in to the 'walls' of the organisation – what theorists refer to as structural capital. It manifests itself in the procedures and ways of working that all individuals share. It incorporates the team spirit or 'culture' of the organisation, and the sense of loyalty and commitment that individuals show for it. It can be thought of as the value that is left behind when the employees or team members go home for the night. Put bluntly, it is the intangible thing that Manchester United has which Chelsea does not.

Among the teams visited by Eriksson in the 1980s when he was starting out as a coach were Liverpool and Ipswich Town, then managed by Sir Bobby Robson who went on to manage England. These were clubs with clearly articulated and carefully cherished values. At Liverpool there was the culture of the 'boot room', the long serving coaches who worked with manager Bob Paisley and who set the club's standards. At Ipswich the culture was that of a small club battling to succeed but battling with a clear idea of how the game should be played. Interestingly, both clubs later lost their way. This could be attributed to them forgetting what had made them great in the first place – and worthy of a visit from an aspiring Swedish coach. Liverpool forgot the values of the boot room while Ipswich briefly forgot the values of loyalty and playing with panache. Once people were appointed as managers who respected the club's traditions – Gerard Houllier at Liverpool and George Burley at Ipswich – the clubs revived and re-discovered themselves.

Viewed in this way, Eriksson's job boils down to two things – picking the right group of players, and then creating the ethos or culture that allows those players to perform their best as a team. His job is in many ways a lot harder than Sir Alex Ferguson's or Arsene Wenger's, because he only gets a slice of his players' time. He does not have the time to create the deep personal relationships and the strong culture that underpins truly great teams. So he keeps things simple – he picks players from only three or four club teams, he emphasises continuity in selection, and he uses a lot of substitutes in friendly matches to get everyone involved. All useful tactics for building up the social fabric of the team when they don't get together very often.

'As a club manager, you work with the players every day and can buy and sell players if you are not happy. When you work with a national team, you must have a good organisation and be very good at picking the right players at the right moment,' Eriksson reflects. 'I have never seen the decisions between 4–4-2 and 4–3-3 as being the most important for a coach … What I want is the right attitude and the best players.'[5]

Making the whole greater than the sum of the parts

How does this apply to the business world? How can you turn your organisation into the Manchester United of your industry? Interestingly there are some business sectors that bear a remarkable resemblance to the sports world – investment banking and consulting, for example, where value is created primarily through the intellectual capital of the employees, and where salaries are by far the highest business expense. The parallels are clear. There is an active transfer market for 'star' analysts, brokers, and consultants. The product is highly intangible, essentially the services provided by a team of highly-paid professionals. It is highly competitive.

Research by Boris Groysberg at Harvard Business School looked at what happened to 'star' analysts when they switched from one investment bank to another.[6] Despite the widespread belief among bankers that the skills of analysts are portable, he discovered that their performance dropped significantly at their new employer. Even analysts, it seems, need an organisation around them to do their job effectively. And more interesting still, Groysberg discovered a big difference across banks in their ability to get their new analysts up to speed – with Merrill Lynch and Goldman Sachs as the best. Merrill and Goldman, in other words, are like Manchester United – they have the culture and the social fabric that helps individuals to excel. The same goes for McKinsey in the consulting industry – a firm that is similar to its peers on most tangible dimensions, but as a collective is consistently ahead of the pack.

Almost by definition, it is a long hard slog to turn yourself into the Manchester United of your industry sector. But there are a few key principles to bear in mind:

- **Nurture talent.** Start nurturing and investing in people from a young age. Manchester United picks out talented kids before they reach their teens. This may not be legal in your industry, but you can certainly target university graduates and school leavers. By investing in their professional development, you kill several birds with one stone – you create loyalty, you reduce the subsequent costs of recruitment, and you can even indulge in a spot of brainwashing (though probably better to call it an orientation programme).

- **Invest in personal development on an ongoing basis.** Coaching does not stop once your employees are in their jobs. By making an ongoing commitment to training and development, you are sending a strong signal to the marketplace about how much you value your human assets. There is an interesting dilemma though, because the more you invest in your people, the easier it is for them to leave. But at the same time, the more you invest in them, the less likely they are to leave.

- **Build up and leverage your networks.** McKinsey, the American consultancy, is well known for aggressively outplacing even high-performing consultants. This ensures there is no stigma associated with leaving. And more to the point, it creates a vast alumni network of executives like IBM's Lou Gerstner and the British politician William Hague, many of whom will seek out McKinsey's services in the years to come. Manchester United has pulled off the same trick – players who spent some time at Old Trafford are highly regarded, and they act as ambassadors for their former club. (When it won the European Champions League in 1999 all former players were invited to the game, even if they only played a handful of games in the dim and distant past.)

- **Take advantage of customer loyalty.** Manchester United has become a truly global brand over the last two decades, and this becomes a great source of value to the club – not just in terms of all the profits that come from merchandising, but also because it makes attracting and retaining top players much easier.

- **Be the best.** Not everyone can do this, of course, but if you can define your business specifically enough that you are the world leader, it creates an enormously powerful magnet for pulling in talent.

The individual and the collective

As with the concepts of empowerment and coaching, the relation- ship between the individual and the team varies with cultural setting. Researchers have traditionally distinguished between individualistic countries like the US where egotistical and self-centred behaviour is accepted, even praised, and collectivist countries like Japan where the team is everything. Britain scores relatively high on individualism, though rather lower than the US. Sweden is middling – more col- lectivist than Anglo-Saxon countries, but more individualist than the Japanese and other oriental countries.

But this distinction misses the point, because the paradox of team behaviour is that both the individual and the team perfomance mat- ter. A study by Ingalill Holmberg and Staffan Åkerblom, two Swedish

When is a team a family?

Office corridors in Britain are full of sporting metaphors – you can be 'batting on a sticky wicket', or you may be 'playing a game of two halves'. Americans are even more obsessed with sports metaphors – they talk about the 'Monday morning quarterback' who analyses prob- lems from afar, or 'Swinging with the bases loaded' when a decision is very important. At the heart of these metaphors is the idea that a busi- ness team has some parallels with a sports team – a group of people, working together, with a coach or manager, against a competitor, and so on. Not only do these metaphors help to simplify or give meaning to a situation, they also help to shape the appropriate action. If the team is a sports team, for example, then competitive rivalry is emphasised.

Two American academics, Cris Gibson and Mary Zellmer-Bruhn, looked at how teams in business settings described their activities, and their use of metaphors. While the sports team was a common metaphor – at least among Anglo Saxon countries – there were also four others – Military, Family, Associates, and Community. Employees in a Philippines-based business, for example, emphasised the community as the way of thinking about the team – the idea that people come together to help community members.

This research has profound implications. As Gibson and Zellmer-Bruhn noted, 'managers cannot assume their own concepts of teamwork will be shared in international settings.' If the employees think of themselves as a competitive sports team, while the manager likens them to a family, conflict and confusion will result'. As for Sweden, Gibson observed that 'Swedish team members would probably have expectations that include broad scope of activities and informal roles – typically the "community" and "associate" metaphors.'

Typical terms used to apply the five metaphors:

- Sports – coach, championship, home run, game, competition.
- Military – battle, campaign, survival, alliances, mobilise.
- Family – brother, family, clannish, father, mother, sister.
- Associates – circle, cliques, council, entity, franchise.
- Community – fraternity, friend, neighbourhood, buddies, Baya.

Source: C. Gibson and M. Zellmer-Bruhn, 'Metaphors and Meaning', *Adminstrative Science Quarterly*, 2001.

researchers, showed that 'Sweden is both an extremely collective and extremely individualistic society'. Individual independence is important, but there is a belief that it can be fulfilled and expressed through society. The individual does not take to the highway on a Harley to set out on a voyage of self-discovery, but seeks to improve things from within with other people. The ultimate Scandinavian driving machine is the solid and safe Volvo.

'If you're an individualist why can't you be a communitarian?' asks Fons Trompenaars, the Dutch management expert. 'Look at the success of the semiconductor industry. They take individualists and form very creative teams out of them. Reconciling such differences is at the heart of our work and of business in the 21st century.'[7]

Sometimes the individual can rise above the occasion. Truly brilliant individualistic performances can secure team success. In England's final World Cup qualifying match against Greece in 2002, the England captain David Beckham gave a bravura performance of intense commitment and skill. At times he appeared to be taking on the entire Greek team alone. His team mates, petrified by nerves, stood and watched. When he scored a last minute equaliser there was a feeling of justice. His performance deserved a finale of substance. Yet, Beckham's team mates were still instrumental in the result – the goalkeeper Nigel Martyn made a series of fine saves.

Even the concept of what a team *is* does not translate readily from one country to another. In a fascinating piece of research, Cris Gibson and Mary Zellmer-Bruhn, two American academics, looked at the way teams were described in different cultures. In America and Britain the dominant metaphor was of course the sports team. But other cultures focused on family, community, or other associates. And far from being a semantic difference, they found that this had an important impact on the sorts of behaviours that people expected of their team members.

Team decision making

Researchers have shown that the combination of individualism and collectivism offers the greatest potential for team success. If people are too individualistic they will sacrifice the team's goals to achieve their own ends. But if people are too collectivist the team will end up wallowing in mediocrity because no-one is prepared to take a strong position. Again, the Swedish model lends itself to effective team dynamics because of the underlying cultural values and norms.

But be warned – Swedish team meetings are not what the average British or American businessman is used to. One of us still has clear memories of his first meeting as a member of Swedish research institute. There was no agenda. People arrived in dribs and drabs, mostly about 15 minutes late. We then had a discussion – a long, rambling discussion about many issues, some clearly important, others not. Arguments were made and counter-arguments put forward, typically in a very straightforward manner. Only very rarely did anyone become defensive. After an hour and a half we concluded the meeting. No summary, no action items, just a general agreement that it had been a good meeting.

For the naïve Englishman newly arrived in Sweden this lack of closure was frustrating, but it quickly became a very attractive part of the Swedish management style. Essentially the meeting was about building consensus. It allowed everyone to air their views. It helped the director to understand who was for or against a particular proposal, and what their reasons were. And it provided him with an opportunity to steer the group towards a mutually agreeable outcome. At the conclusion of the meeting there was no need for a formal summary because everyone – except the Englishman in the corner – knew what had been decided. The meeting was also only one part of the decision-making process – there were individual conversations beforehand, and there would be others afterwards. A drawn-out process, to be sure, but one that ensured much greater buy-in than the typical business meeting.

So what are the elements of group decision-making, Swedish style? Here are some key attributes:

- **Consensus building.** Everyone has an opinion, and a right to air that opinion. It is often stated in Ericsson, the telecom equipment company, that 'a decision by a senior manager is an interesting input into the discussion'. The comment is partially tongue-in-cheek of course, but it hints at an underlying culture of consensus-building in the company. Robin Peddlar, Associate Fellow at Templeton College, Oxford, trained the Swedish government for the EU presidency in 2001. As he recalled, 'when asked about their style of working, they typically emphasised their sharing approach – for example, business, unions and governments working together.'

    Consensus and negotiation are essential are at the heart of Swedish leadership. 'Consensus is seen as a condition for dialogue and also as a preferred outcome of the dialogue,' say Ingalill Holmberg and Staffan Åkerblom of the Stockholm School of Economics.

'The Swedish management style is very consensus based. The CEO spends a lot of time trying to get agreement. Swedish executives are never surprised by a CEO decision,' says Lars Nyberg, CEO of NCR.

- **Empathy.** Swedes, as we discussed earlier, are strong on the feminine values of supporting, nurture and empathising with one another. And they dislike the grandstanding behaviour often seen in more masculine cultures like the US. Good team members listen carefully, seek to understand and empathise with their colleagues' point of view.

- **Straight-talking.** Paradoxically, the Swedes are also very straightforward and pragmatic people. Percy Barnevik, former CEO of ABB, was well known for his rather brusque manner and his decisiveness. If a Swede disagrees with his colleague, he will tell him, straight. If an Englishman disagrees with his colleague, he will typically talk around the issue, illuminating alternative perspectives and so forth, but never actually saying what he wants to say. Straight-talking is a key factor in effective discussions, as long as it stays at a professional level. Intel, the American microprocessor company, even has a term for this – *constructive confrontation*. As explained by John McGowan, head of Intel in Ireland, 'this is not about having a big shouting match, it is simply seen as a way of airing contrary views, to try to avoid political games'.

- **Honesty.** Old fashioned virtues are in. Typically, in one survey, American executives rated honesty as the prime business virtue; Swedish executives did not include honesty at all – it was assumed. 'Our business is built on trust. A handshake is a handshake,' says Jan Lapidoth. 'This means that we keep legalities to a minimum. We talk to each other, settle it and get on with it.'

- **Informality.** Swedish society is very egalitarian and this is reflected in the informal style of meetings. Typically, meetings are opened up to a broad base of people, and everyone is invited to contribute to the discussion. As one South American manager observed: 'When observing a group of Swedish people, figuring out which one is the boss is more difficult since people at all different levels in the organisation can speak more or less freely.'

Warren Bennis on great teams

When it comes to leadership few have contributed more to our under-standing than the American Warren Bennis. Bennis' latest work focuses on the interaction between leaders and their teams. We asked him to explain.

Do great groups require great leaders?

Bennis: Greatness starts with superb people. Great groups don't exist without great leaders, but they give the lie to the persistent notion that successful institutions are the lengthened shadow of a great woman or man. It's not clear that life was ever so simple that individuals, acting alone, solved most significant problems. None of us is as smart as all of us.

So, the John Wayne type of hero is of the past?

Bennis: Yes, the Lone Ranger is dead. Instead of the individual prob-lem solver we have a new model for creative achievement. People like Steve Jobs or Walt Disney headed groups and found their own great-ness in them. The new leader is a pragmatic dreamer, a person with an original but attainable vision. Ironically, the leader is able to realize his or her dream only if the others are free to do exceptional work. Typi-cally, the leader is the one who recruits the others, by making the vision so palpable and seductive that they see it, too, and eagerly sign up.

Inevitably, the leader has to invent a leadership style that suits the group. The standard models, especially command and control, simply don't work. The heads of groups have to act decisively, but never ar-bitrarily. They have to make decisions without limiting the perceived autonomy of the other participants. Devising and maintaining an at-mosphere in which others can put a dent in the universe is the leader's creative act.

But isn't this somewhat unrealistic?

Bennis: True. Most organisations are dull, and working life is mundane. There is no getting away from that. So, these groups could be an inspiration. A great group is more than a collection of first-rate minds. It's a miracle. I have unwarranted optimism. By looking at the possibilities we can all improve.

What will it take for future leaders to be effective?

Bennis: The post-bureaucratic organisation requires a new kind of alliance between leaders and the led. Today's organisations are evolving into federations, networks, clusters, cross-functional teams, temporary systems, ad hoc task forces, lattices, modules, matrices – almost anything but pyramids with their obsolete top-down leadership. The new leader will encourage healthy dissent and values those followers courageous enough to say no.

This does not mark the end of leadership – rather the need for a new, far more subtle and indirect form of influence for leaders to be effective. The new reality is that intellectual capital (brain power, know-how, and human imagination) has supplanted capital as the critical success factor; and leaders will have to learn an entirely new set of skills that are not understood, not taught in our business schools, and, for all of those reasons, rarely practised.

Notes

1 Interview with George Yip, 28 September 2001.
2 Campbell, Denis, 'The history man', *The Observer*, 13 January 2002.
3 Scase, Richard, 'The Swede smell of success', www.londonbusinessforum.com, 15 October 2001.
4 Author interview.
5 Anthony, Andrew, 'Svengland', *The Observer*, 5 August 2001.

6 Groysberg, Boris, 'Can they take it with them?', Doctoral thesis, Harvard Business School, 2002.
7 Author interview.

KEEP IT SIMPLE

9

'There are no big egos around the
England camp because he has no
ego himself. I love watching him
work. He makes the game simple. His
explanations are not cluttered with
detail. He gets his message across
with a minimum of complications
and the players respond.'

– Eriksson's chief scout, Dave Sexton,
ex-manager of Manchester United.[1]

Controlling fuss

I n Kevin Keegan's final game, the England team played like strangers. It was as if they had not spent the previous week passing the ball to each other. Indeed, this was a characteristic of other of their performances under Keegan. The players simply did not appear to know what each other was doing. Usually reliable passers of the ball would unerringly find a member of the opposition team. One explanation of this can be seen by a look at the team sheet of the game against Germany. Included in the England team was the defender Gareth Southgate. Southgate is an intelligent person and a highly experienced footballer. Against Germany he was asked to play in the unfamiliar territory of midfield. His performance left a lot to be desired. If Southgate had a natural ability to play as a midfielder, he would have been playing there for his club. In unfamiliar territory, Southgate looked bemused. The game passed him by.

Sven-Göran Eriksson's approach to team strategy rests on a few simple premises. The England team don't get a lot of time together, so players play in the position they are most accustomed to in their club side. The basic 4–4-2 formation is kept constant. Team selection is – to the extent that it is possible – kept the same from game to game.

'One bad thing is there are too few games and too few practices, so you really don't have time to do a lot', says Eriksson. 'So when you realise that I think you pick the best players and let them do what they are good at doing, let them play in the position they normally play in. I don't have time to try playing Beckham in the centre.'[2]

Unlike some previous managers, Eriksson does his homework, decides on his formation, his key players, and sticks with them. Simplicity rules.

'He has a firm view on the right way to play. In essence, formations are just numbers. He has faith in the system and understands what we're trying to do,' says David Platt who was brought in as England Under 21 coach under Eriksson – Platt also played for Eriksson at Sampdoria.[3]

Interestingly, Eriksson was converted to the 4–4-2 formation through the work of two English coaches in his native Sweden. In the

1980s Bob Houghton at Malmo and Roy Hodgson at Halmstad were successful in introducing a more English-style approach in Sweden. This, in turn, had been inspired by the success of Liverpool – a club greatly admired by Eriksson. The basic formula was for a 'pressing' style with players pressuring the opposition as quickly as possible and passing the ball forward as quickly as possible with a minimum of fuss.

Keeping it simple means cutting out external factors which get in the way of great performance. In effect, it means focusing on the simple things you excel at. This is harder than it sounds. In the football world over complication is the mark of any number of teams. The current Chelsea team, for example, boasts a world-beating array of World Cup winners and world class players. And yet, the Chelsea coach, Claudio Ranieri, 'the tinkerman', has a relentless urge to change things, to make team patterns more complex. The players often play as if the complexity has overwhelmed them. They don't know what is expected of them and, as a result, cannot perform to the best of their abilities.

In the business world the temptation to tinker and change, to add more, is often irresistible. Companies expand madly and thoughtlessly into more and more different areas until, eventually, they forget what made them successful in the first place. It is far harder to rein things in, to keep things simple when faced with wave after wave of complexity.

Keeping it simple is the basic strategy pursued by the Finnish telecoms giant Nokia.

Jorma Ollila became Nokia's CEO in 1992. Ollila took a 147-year-old company comprised of an assortment of businesses from timber to rubber boots and transformed it into a mobile phone colossus. Ollila simplified the company, ditching non-core activities like the paper, rubber, cable, computer and TV businesses. In 1998, it passed the US company Motorola as the world's No. 1 mobile-phone manufacturer. In less than eight years Ollila made Nokia the most valuable company in Europe.

Ollila has also applied his talent for simplicity to the company's branding. He abandoned the existing array of mobile phone brands produced by Nokia, concentrating on a product line emblazoned with the Nokia name. Internally, he cut out bureaucracy. Out went hierarchical management structures; in came a flat organisational structure. Today things get done in the company through networks of individuals. It's an entrepreneurial, innovative environment within a large corporation. Then there is the Nokia Way – a means of tapping into root feeling at the company. Brainstorming at a series of meetings throughout the company is synthesised into a vision statement by the top managers, and this is disseminated back through the organisation via a series of presentations. The Nokia Way keeps the employees plugged in to the company.

Lessons from the army

Keeping it simple does not necessarily mean sticking with the same strategy forever. In fact, it really means the exact reverse. Consider this logic. No football coach can know how the game is going to unfold. And no business leader can create a grand strategy in which every new technology and every competitive move is anticipated. So rather than attempt to predict an unknowable future, the master strategist defines some basic parameters and rules, provides his team with the skills and awareness they need, and then lets them get on with the job.

The British Army provide a good example of this model. Military strategy is continuously evolving – from the trench warfare of the First World War to the aerial bombardments and Blitzkreigs of the Second, to the stalemate of the Cold War. Then the Berlin Wall came down, and the British Army had to contemplate an uncertain future. Through a process called the Strategic Defence Review the Army looked at the changing nature of armed conflict, and the sorts of wars they would have to be prepared to fight in a one-superpower world. And they came up with a surprising model.

Out went the old command-and-control doctrine, in which orders were given and followed without justification. In its place they created a fluid, more flexible model in which commanders were given instructions on what was to be achieved, and not how it should be done. The commander should understand not just his orders, but those one or two levels up, so that he can use his own judgement on how to adapt to the changing situation on the battlefield. In the words of Major Philip Barber, the commander position 'calls for an attitude of mind in which doing the unexpected and seeking originality is combined with a ruthless determination to succeed'.

This approach was designed around the changing nature of conflict. Wars, the Army reasoned, were more likely to be fought in mountainous areas or jungles than the plains and deserts of the Second World War, and the enemy would be shadowy and indeterminate. So a style known as the 'manoeuvrist approach' was developed, based on an earlier German theory called *Aufstragtaktik*. This approach was built around momentum and tempo. The defeat of the enemy would be achieved by disrupting their command system, and by applying pressures just when it is least expected. And it worked by giving commando units some straightforward rules to follow and then leaving them to figure out how to adapt those rules to the rapidly-evolving circumstances on the ground.

The business world is starting to figure out the benefits of simple rules for strategy making. Kathleen Eisenhardt and Don Sull, two American business school professors, argue that, paradoxically, complex times call for simple rules. As they put it, 'managers know that the greatest opportunities for competitive advantage lie in market confusion, so they jump into chaotic martkets, probe for opportunities, build on succesful forays, and shift flexibly among opportunities as circumstances dictate. But they recognise the need for a few key strategic processes to help them through the chaos'.

Swedish management – with its emphasis on empowerment and informality – has for a long time been built around the logic of 'simple rules'. Tetra Pak, the liquid carton company founded by the Rausing brothers, used to send bright young managers in their twenties and thirties out to foreign markets with the basic equipment for making the product and some financial targets. How they developed the market was their problem, but sure enough many were highly successful.

Similarly, when Percy Barnevik created ABB's famous matrix organisation the intention was to liberate, rather than constrain, its managers. Essentially it worked by decentralising decision making to over one thousand separate business units. Instead of worrying about the complexities of being part of a global corporation, each business would concentrate on its own local customers and its own assets, and the task of knitting together this federation of businesses would fall to a small number of global executives.

Simple rules, complex outcomes

There is an underlying theory here that builds on the esoteric world of complexity science. Think of the weather. While meteorologists understand the underlying science pretty well these days, they struggle to predict exactly how a weather system will evolve because small differences in the starting conditions can result in massive differences in final outcomes, because of the way the different factors interact with each other. Indeed, in modelling complex systems like the weather, it becomes apparent that a simple set of rules can produce highly complex and evolved end states. And this logic does not apply only to pure science. Researchers have studied the complex 'towns' that ants build – complete with homes, food stores and cemeteries – and they have concluded that these sophisticated social systems arise not because the ants have particularly high levels of intelligence but because they are programmed to follow a few simple rules.

It may sound like a bit of a stretch to apply observations about the weather and ants to management, but the nucleus of the idea is very powerful. Give people clear rules, and clear boundaries. Provide them with enough structure that they will work together, but enough freedom that they will experiment. And leave them to it. Jazz improvisation is another powerful metaphor for describing this. As Shona Brown and Kathy Eisenhardt describe in their book *Competing on the Edge:* 'Improvisation is challenging to achieve because it is so easy to err on either side – to slip into too much structure or too little. In complexity theory terms, improvisation is … an unstable edge between two attractors (i.e. structure and chaos) that tend to pull the system away from the edge of chaos… and yet staying on that edge is essential because that is where systems self-organise to create the most vibrant, adaptive and complex behaviours.'

If successful strategies emerge from the 'self-organising' efforts of individual employees, what is the role left for the leader? Is Sven-Göran Eriksson abdicating his responsibilities if all he does is define some basic parameters and then lets his players get on with developing strategy themselves?

Academics have debated this point in a variety of settings, and they have typically concluded that the opposite is the case – that most key decisions actually 'belong' to the players, so when the manager makes decisions he is often taking responsibility for *their* decisions. The Catholic church, for example, states that 'it is an injustice, a grave evil, for a large and higher organisation to arrogate to itself functions which can be performed efficiently by smaller and lower bodies'. In politics the term subsidiarity is used to mean the same thing – that the higher order body (e.g. the European Union) should only become involved when the lower order bodies (e.g. the UK or France) believe some form of collective action is appropriate. Even if it does not really work this way in practice, the principle is sound, and it works pretty well in truly federal countries like Canada and the US.

British management thinker Charles Handy sums up this concept in a single sentence – 'stealing people's responsibilities is wrong'. Good management is about leaving your team to make their own decisions, allowing them to learn through their mistakes, and knowing when to intervene.

So what is the leader's role in shaping strategy? Essentially it boils down to these five elements:

- **Set direction.** What is your objective? For Sven-Göran Eriksson, it is clear enough – to win the World Cup. For most businesses there are multiple overlapping and contradictory objectives, so the leader has to prioritise among them and communicate to his employees where she believes they should be heading. Sometimes the direction is stated in very clear terms. Ericsson, the Swedish telecoms giant, defined its objective a couple of years ago as 'establishing a leading role in the new telecoms world' based on its wireless networking technologies. Direction setting can also be much more vague – Ingvar Kamprad, the founder of IKEA, spoke about his determination to 'create a better everyday life for the majority of people'.
- **Define the boundaries.** As well as indicating a broad direction in which to head, leaders also have to articulate the out-of-bounds areas. The England football team has to stay within the rules of the beautiful game, and Eriksson also lays the law down about behav-

iour off the pitch. In business there are a plethora of legal, moral and ethical rules. There are also typically business areas that are simply beyond the boundaries of the company's expertise. Ericsson is open-minded when it comes to new business development (after trying to kill off its mobile phone business multiple times in the early 1990s) but it is clear that all ventures have to be within the 'new telecoms world'.

- **Home in on your simple rules.** This is the tricky bit, because no-one can tell you what your simple rules should be. Sven-Goran Eriksson's rules are based around the 4–4-2 formation, the particular roles given to certain key players, and the preference to have everyone in their usual position. In the business context, rules can take many forms – they can focus on key processes, or prioritising options. Eisenhardt and Sull's research offers some thoughts (see box). The best approach is typically to figure out what you have started to do anyway (through trial and error) and formalise that.

- **Let the employees get on with it.** Once the three elements above are in place, the best thing the leader can do is give his people space. Watch Sven-Göran Eriksson on the touchline during England matches. He is focused, intense, and involved, but he is not yelling at the players from the touchline. And he does not spend his half-time talk reworking the game plan, changing tactics and positions.

- **Provide support.** Support refers to the training and development people are given so that they are able to make the right judgment when faced with a tricky situation. It also involves having peer support – colleagues who can offer advice and help on the basis of their own experiences. BP has taken this idea further than most by developing 'peer support groups' in which businesses have the obligation to help the others within their peer group improve their performance.

The dark side of simplicity

The keep it simple approach to strategy is not for those of a nervous disposition. As we discussed earlier, it means giving employees enough freedom that they can fail. And it means not meddling at the first signs of trouble. But at the same time leadership does not mean abdicating responsibility. If mistakes are made, the leader will ultimately be called in to sort out the mess.

Herein lies the great challenge of the keep it simple strategy.

To work, it relies on employees taking initiative – acting entrepreneurially and creatively within their boundaries. But at the same time, initiative is about taking risks, and entrusting employees to act without supervision. What if they go too far? What if they start pursuing empire-building strategies that help no-one but themselves? What if they take excessive risks?

The recent history of business is littered with cases of companies that gave too much freedom to their employees. Nick Leeson brought down Barings Bank through his derivative trading exploits in Singapore. Joseph Jett almost did the same to Kidder Peabody, an American bank. And several recent corporate scandals, including Enron, World-Com and Parmalat, stemmed from the creative-but-illicit actions of its executives.

Sven yourself: choosing your simple rules

In a turbulent, fast-changing world, successful companies are the ones that focus on a few simple rules within which employees are free to act. There are five basic types of rules:

- **How-to rules** – that define the key features of how a process is executed.
- **Boundary rules** – that focus employees on which opportunities they can pursue and which to avoid.
- **Priority rules** – that help employees to rank their interesting opportunities.
- **Timing rules** – that synchronise employees with the pace of opportunities in the marketplace and with other parts of the company.
- **Exit rules** – that help employees to decide what businesses to quit and when.

Source: Eisenhardt and Sull, *Harvard Business Review*, 2001.

These examples highlight what we might call the dark side of entrepreneurship. Like anything else, entrepreneurship is a valuable attribute in moderation, but when it is taken too far it creates risks. Four in particular:

- **Risk of lack of focus.** Some companies take the approach that you should 'let a thousand flowers bloom' in new idea development. All well and good, but if this is taken too far, the coherence that strategy needs is lost. A clear direction, and rules for prioritising opportunities, are needed to avoid this problem.
- **Risk of duplication of effort.** A related problem is when several people end up solving the same problem. This is the essence of the market system, where similar products end up vying for the customer's attention. But inside a single company too much duplication in effort is just waste.
- **Risk of opportunism.** Most people are honest and trustworthy, but there are always a few rats – individuals who will find ways of making a personal profit at the expense of their employer. The problem is figuring out who they are. 'The difference between genius and madness' argued Elliot Carver, the evil media baron in the James Bond movie *Tomorrow Never Dies*, 'is measured only by the end result'. The same logic applies here – the opportunistic employee looks remarkably like the well-intentioned entrepreneur until the results of their actions are known.
- **Risk that initiative drives out day-to-day work.** The fact is, being creative and entrepreneurial is a lot more fun than doing your everyday job. So if too much emphasis is placed on initiative, it can easily get in the way of the more routine parts of your work.

Leading paradoxically

You may still be uncomfortable with the notion of keeping it simple. The most likely reason for this is that you see complexity lurking at every corner. How can simplicity be made to work in such a complex environment?

In truth it is a juggling act. Yet, it is this juggling act which lies at the heart of leadership the Sven-Göran Eriksson way. It is the ability to cope with and communicate the nature of such paradoxes that is the core of leadership. Modern leaders have to embrace the paradoxical combination of simplicity and complexity.

One of the most thoughtful of CEOs is Nino Vella of the brilliantly named, New Pig Corporation, based in Tipton, Pennsylvania. Vella argues that management is now beset by a series of paradoxes – such as the more successful you are, the nearer to failure you become. Management, therefore, is concerned with managing such paradoxes.

'Pinning your hopes on a single future scenario is foolish. You have to head off in different directions simultaneously,' says Vella. 'Along the way things will change. The worth of a vision, a plan, and a statement does not lie in its shelf life. The pursuit of serial futures requires that you head off, do something, check how it impacts reality, then change. Then you do it again. You check it out, you change. Whenever you put a plan or vision together you aren't tied to it for life. You might discover something just when your plan is complete which completely invalidates it.'[4]

Vella admits that, to some, this constitutes weak leadership. The iron-fisted corporate tyrant of the past was unlikely to change his mind at the last minute. CEOs were not for turning. 'In reality, opposing such change and contradiction is where the true danger lies. When change is constant, our approach to the future and our understanding of what it holds must be constantly changing. And, if the future is changing, then we're going to get it wrong. This not something managers are used to accepting, but accept it they must,' says Nino Vella before going on to map out the one certainty amid the paradoxes, 'Some things don't change and those things are our values. For companies without values the future is a minefield in the dark.'

The ability to let go while retaining control, to simplify while accepting inherent complexity, is very close to the essence of Sweden. 'The Swedes have unknowingly, and ironically with increasing skill, during the last century practiced what I refer to as a radical pragmatics in their way of handling complex issues such as leadership,' says Alexander Bard. 'And hardly nobody practices this concept better in real life than Eriksson. A radical pragmatic in leadership can be incredibly successful not only on the football field, but also when it comes to handling other organisations founded on a basic paradox. A similar situation that comes to mind is the organisation of soldiers on a peace mission, another Scandinavian speciality. To organise soldiers, trained to fight to death and always carrying heavy weaponry, to enforce and uphold peace, that most fragile of social categories, leaves no room for strategies of stability as in traditional ideologies. It can only work successfully in a state of radical pragmatics, a firm leadership still fluent in mobility. This is exactly what Eriksson practices on the football field. As a football trainer, he is the radical pragmatist par excellence.'[5] Radical pragmatists of the world unite.

Notes

1 Draper, Ron, 'How Sven plotted quiet revolution', www.soccernet.com
2 Interview with George Yip, 28 September 2001.
3 Draper, Ron, 'How Sven plotted quiet revolution', www.soccernet.com
4 Author interview.
5 Author interview.

10
NEVER WALK ALONE

'Tord gave me my start and gave me the best schooling I could ever have had.'

– Sven-Göran Eriksson[1]

The leader's loneliness

We spend a lot of our time talking to senior executives. All complain of the stress and pressure. But, when we talk to people at the very top of corporations the chief complaint is not the pressure or the workload – these are expected – but the loneliness. Leadership is a lonely job.

A typical view comes from Katherine Hammer president and CEO of the Austin, Texas-based Evolutionary Technologies International. 'There are some people who do it all themselves. But most of us depend on other people. It is a hard job. I look at people running huge companies and I don't know how they cope. Executive pay may look exorbitant, but look at the responsibilities,' she says. 'It does help to have someone to talk to, to have a sounding board. Sometimes I'll ask someone from another company. People are very generous with their time if you want advice on a targeted issue.

'I think there are three stages in professional development. In the first you are an apprentice, looking for a mentor. You work hard waiting for someone to tap you on the shoulder – but that doesn't happen to most people. Then you become frustrated and more willing to take on additional risk. At this stage you are apt to fight more and express anger. In the third stage you begin to learn how to deal with hard things such as how to bank your anger. This job's taught me the need to bank your anger in order to be more effective.'[2]

Other CEOs echo such comments. 'Every CEO needs to be able to go to someone who doesn't know the business. I have a mentor who is based in Dallas and who is a sounding board for the issues I have to deal with. By putting things in writing it can be helpful. Being a CEO needn't be a lonely process,' says Mike Day, CEO of Indicater.com.[3] 'Being a CEO is less and less fun just when it is harder and harder for corporates to evolve fast enough to stay alive,' laments Richard Nissen, former CEO of the Virtual Office. 'The CEO's job gets to be more and more miserable as most of the staff are against you most of the time. Managers all feel it is their job to be testeronic and aggressive (tough negotiators, etc.), so that areas of co-operation with suppliers and other partners are often subverted by aggressive behaviour – 'the other side is always wrong' syndrome. 'Meanwhile the CEO is the skipper trying to keep the ship afloat in huge storms and steering in the right direction. Ultimately, like the captain, the CEO is responsible for everything yet he has no disciplinary power to insist on doing it his way.'[4]

The loneliness at the top is real and worsening. Executive coach Dusty Staub spends a lot of time helping executives pick up the pieces. 'There are different ways of coping. Some drink. Some buy lots of expensive toys. They can get pretty lonely. It is very political and usually they don't have a wide network of friends and few confidantes. Their direct reports often filter information.'[5]

In some ways the job of CEO has become too big for a single person. Only a superman could do the job demanded by investors, the media, employees and the market. Those who manage to survive and thrive do so because they recognise that doing everything is impossible. They need to share the responsibility. As we have seen, this is something Sven-Göran Eriksson – and Swedish managers generally – are very adept at.

But more than that, leaders need to work closely with someone they can totally trust. In his trusty lieutenant Tord Grip, Eriksson has that partner. What makes the relationship somewhat unusual is that the older man – Grip is ten years older than Eriksson – is in the junior position.

'Tord's a very capable instructor and very clever at analysing opponents – the best coach in the world,' says Sven-Göran Eriksson.[6]

Their relationship stretches back to 1973 when Grip was the coach at Karlskoga. Then the two worked together for the first time at Degerfors where Eriksson was Grip's assistant.

Grip's departure in 1976 to become the national team's assistant coach opened the door for Eriksson to take charge. While Eriksson cut a swathe through European management, Grip's career followed an idiosyncratic pattern. He became technical director at Malmo in 1981 and later coached the Norwegian national team before a spell in Switzerland with the Young Boys team. In 1992 he became Sweden's assistant coach before eventually rejoining Eriksson at Lazio in 1997.

The relationship with Grip is central to Eriksson's leadership style. 'He always has someone by his side whom he can trust completely, someone who is not looking out to take his job, and with whom he can try out any kind of idea,' says the Swedish author Carl Hamilton.[7]

It takes two

The Eriksson/Grip partnership is also emulated in the business word. Corporate superheroes are usually celebrated for their individuality. They are bright – or lucky – and successful. But, if you look a little deeper, their success stories are usually not about individuals, but about teams and, more frequently, partnerships.

Business partnerships come in all shapes and sizes. Some are official, some are flexible, some are short-term, some are long-term, some work and some bite the dust. Often the partnerships are a combination of opposites. The high profile, risk taker may work with a cautious financier. The marketing genius works in tandem with the arch strategist. The trouble is that there are no hard and fast rules to what works and what doesn't work. The chemistry of business partnerships is as complex and elusive as any human relationship.

'When there is an attraction of whatever kind between two people it seems to be accompanied by a desire to improve – to come up with new ideas, achieve more, make more money,' says Phil Hodgson of Ashridge. 'Sometimes there is also a competitive element with partners producing higher performance from each other than they would achieve individually.' Business partnerships are not, Hodgson quickly points out, the commercial equivalent of marriage. 'In marriage the attraction is – usually – the most important thing. In a business partnership, the emphasis is on the outcome. Partnership is a means of doing something. The partners may not even like each other.'[8]

Even if they more closely resemble marriages of convenience than true romances, the potential to strike it rich is enormous. Going solo has its limitations. When the going gets tough you need someone to turn to and, no matter what the business, you always need someone you can trust and depend on. Little wonder that behind many business successes, there is another success story lurking in the background.

History has proved that some partnerships are made in corporate heaven. Others owe more to corporate hell.

Arsene Wenger and Pat Rice

Arsene Wenger is remarkably similar to Eriksson in his apparent make-up and approach to leadership. 'Although himself a player of only average competence, there is no doubt among players, supporters or in the higher echelons of football, that Arsene (the Professor) Wenger knows every technical aspect of the game. In commanding such an encyclopaedic knowledge of the game – young and gifted players such as Thierry Henry and Robert Pires have flourished and been voted footballers of the year by their French peers,' says Gerry Griffin, author of *The Power Game*, Arsenal devotee and a Wenger admirer. 'Wenger distinguishes himself from the gum-chewing, high-blood pressure antics of classic British managers such as Alex Ferguson, by presenting a cool, intellectual veneer to the tabloid hacks looking to trip him up.

Wearing a wry smile and engaging in the occasional *jeu de mot*, this multi-lingual Frenchman is rumoured never to descend to half-time barrackings in the dressing-room. Instead, he believes that each player should be responsible for his own levels of motivation. Wenger assembles his team with surgical precision – leading to breathtaking displays of football technique (when it works) and the converse when it doesn't.

In many respects, Wenger has been at the vanguard of the foreign manager – paving the way for the likes of Gerrard Houllier and Jean Tigana. This new style takes account of every aspect of the game: Wenger re-designed Arsenal's training ground and facilities (now ranked as one of the finest in Europe). He also sought the replace the less than excellent traditional diets of booze and fast food with pasta and vitamins. The competitive edge which his players display as a result is based on stamina and sheer athleticism. Those yellowed photographs of players celebrating a victory in the fags and lager look more of a different era than ever.'[9]

And who works with Wenger as his assistant? Not a cerebral Frenchman, but a former Arsenal captain, Pat Rice, who has all the vociferous passion and connections with the club which Wenger lacks. In combination the two are far more powerful than if either worked alone.

William Hewlett and David Packard

California registered historical landmark number 976 is a garage in

Palo Alto, California. This is the birthplace of Silicon Valley where college friends Hewlett and Packard began their business in 1938. Their early work included an automatic lettuce thinner, a shock machine to help people lose weight and an optical device which flushed urinals automatically. Hewlett-Packard is now an enormously successful company with hundreds of thousands of employees and billions of dollars in sales. Along the way Hewlett and Packard remained close friends, holidaying and operating ranches together.

Brian Clough and Peter Taylor

The brilliant player and the journeyman; the vocal one and the quiet one. The match of Clough and Taylor proved hugely successful during the 1970s and 1980s in converting two small time clubs, Derby County and Nottingham Forest, into the best sides in Europe. Clough grabbed the headlines with gusto while Taylor stayed quietly in the background. The indifferent performances of the two clubs since the duo's departures shed more light on their achievements.

Bill Gates and Paul Allen/Bill Gates and Steve Ballmer

While still students at a private school in Seattle, Bill Gates and Paul Allen set up their first company. They went on to found Microsoft. Allen, three years older than Gates, left Microsoft in 1983 after an illness and now spends his time overseeing various investments in a basketball team, charities and companies, as well as playing the guitar. 'Paul has gone his own way, but we still see this stuff the same way, and we debate about it and share ideas quite a bit,' says Gates who remains resolutely charting the technological future with Microsoft. Gates knows the value of partnerships. He is now on his second 'marriage'. His partner-in-chief is now the Microsoft CEO Steve Ballmer.

Hans Rausing and Gad Rausing

Born in southern Sweden in the 1920s, Hans and Gad Rausing took control of their father's company, Tetra Pak, in 1954 with Hans as

CEO and Gad as Vice-CEO. Essentially it was a one-product company – the Tetra 'brick' for packaging milk, juice and other liquids. But the brothers exploited this innovation with such speed and technological prowess that they completely dominated the global market. They worked in partnership for 27 years, by which time their personal wealth – estimated at around £4 billion each – placed them among the richest ten individuals in Europe.

Kjell Nordström and Jonas Ridderstråle

Swedish management gurus come in neatly packaged, shaven headed packages of two. The stars of the Swedish guru scene in recent years are the two charismatic academics (co-authors of *Funky Business* and *Karaoke Capitalism*). Their stagecraft owes more to show business than the boardroom but their message – and their manner – has proved an international success. Partnership has a funky side.

The Sven and Tord show

One of the notable things about Kevin Keegan's reign as England coach was that he had no one really close to him, someone who he shared important decisions with. Yes, he had a coaching team including people like Arthur Cox and Derek Fazackerly who had worked with him before, but there was no clear sounding board, no-one standing next to Keegan sharing the burden. (Keegan's predecessor, Glenn Hoddle, had John Gorman as his assistant.)

The Swedish team is managed by Tommy Soderberg and Lars Lagerback. 'Running a national team is not a one man show,' says Soderberg.[10]

With Eriksson there is a clear feeling of there being more than one person involved. Eriksson is the leader, but he has forged valuable partnerships – such as with Tord Grip, and previously with FA CEO Adam Crozier before he left to run the Royal Mail.

Qualities you need in a partner:

- **Complementary skills.** Great leaders – as we discussed in Chapter 3 – have great self awareness. They know what they do well, and they also know where there limitations lie. So the first priority in picking a partner is to look for complementary skills. Hans Snook, former CEO of Orange was a charismatic, visionary and – some would say – eccentric leader. His partner, Graham Howe was a much more traditional manager, but far better at the practical details of running a large and successful business. Steve Jobs, the visionary founder of Apple hired John Sculley from Pepsi in 1981 to provide the marketing capabilities he lacked. (The partnership didn't work. This suggests that finding the right chemistry is more of a vague art than a precise science.)

In many ways this follows the tough cop, nice cop stereotype. Two similar people with similar skills and perspectives rarely work in combination. Starsky & Starsky doesn't work.

- **Share the same values and principles.** Complementary skills are critical, but for partnerships to survive in the long term they have to be based on shared values and principles. Otherwise conflicts will emerge. Sir John Browne, CEO of BP, and Rodney Chase, his former deputy, are very different personalities but they share a fundamental belief in the importance of BP becoming a force for good.

- **Acceptance that there is a boss.** Partnerships sound great and utopian but unless there is a clear delineation of responsibility they will not work. In football coaching, partnerships have usually proved short-lived. At Liverpool Gerrard Houllier was brought in alongside Roy Evans with both designated as joint managers. It didn't work and Evans left. Other clubs have tried similar arrangements with poor results. In the business world, most attempts at power-sharing fail. When Citibank merged with Travelers group, John Reed and Sandy Weill agreed to be co-chairs, but this arrangement only lasted a couple of years before Reed was forced out.

- **Honest feedback.** There has to be a great degree of openness and frankness for any relationship to work. The deputy has to feel confident enough to speak out if concerned. 'I think we share the same principles about football but if I disagree with something, yes, I will tell him,' says Tord Grip.[11] While Eriksson reflects: 'Tord is incredibly important. When you are moving teams and countries, you need someone alongside you who you know and who you can be confident will be honest with you.'[12]

Sven yourself

The Eriksson/Grip type of relationship is most often seen in a business situation when a more senior executive mentors a younger or less senior executive (though mentoring can also involve someone more experienced offering help to a less experienced leader).

Linda Phillips-Jones, one of the leading experts on mentoring, describes mentors as 'skilled people who go out of their way to help you clarify your personal goals and take steps toward reaching them.' In her book *Mentors and Protégés* she describes some characteristics of mentors and the mentoring relationship:[13]

- Mentors are usually older than their protégés.
- Mentors frequently – but not always – initiate the relationship.
- Mentor–protégé relationships do not need to be particularly close.
- It is possible to have more than one mentor at a time.
- There are patterns and cycles in mentor-protégé relationships.
- Mentoring should benefit both partners equally.

A good mentor can:

- expand your horizons and perspectives
- help build your confidence and give you moral support
- provide you with a professional role model
- improve your skills level, and emotional and intellectual development
- provide you with professional connections, and acquaint you with industry-specific values and customs
- provide objective feedback on a performance
- help you enter and advance within your chosen career.

Mentors can be very useful in relieving one of the most significant factors in determining job satisfaction – stress. According to Linda Hill, consultant and Harvard Business School academic, even the most experienced managers often report feelings of conflict, ambiguity and isolation. 'The myriad of challenges encountered when one becomes a manager are difficult to shoulder alone,' Unfortunately, new managers can be reluctant to ask for help; it doesn't fit their conception of the boss as expert.'[14]

The mentor's role varies according a variety of factors, including the quality of the relationship between mentors and the mentee, the level of skills and knowledge of both parties, time available, and organisational culture.

In the various literature on mentoring a number of specific roles associated with mentors have been identified:

- acceptor
- counsellor
- coach
- challenger
- friend
- listener
- promoter
- inquisitor
- protector
- role model
- sponsor.

The perfect mentor, someone who can assume all of the roles above, probably does not exist. Rather than pursuing a fruitless quest to find the perfect mentor you would be better advised to assess which type will be most valuable to you, and then look for a mentor that embodies those qualities. It also pays to learn how to become a perfect mentee, so that mentors will want to take you on. Realistically assess whether you are an attractive proposition to a mentor. Are you ambitious, willing to confide in others, willing to learn? If you're not then why should a mentor give up their valuable time to help you?

Notes

1 Fletcher, Paul, 'Eriksson's iron grip', BBC Sport Web site, http://news.bbc.co.uk/sport, 9 January 2002.
2 Author interview.
3 Author interview.
4 Author interview.

5 Author interview.
6 Fletcher, Paul, 'Eriksson's iron grip', BBC Sport Web site, http://news.bbc.co.uk/sport, 9 January 2002.
7 Author interview.
8 Author interview.
9 Author interview.
10 Fletcher, Paul, 'Sweden's dream team', BBC Sport Web site, http://news.bbc.co.uk/sport, 3 November 2001.
11 FA Web site www.the-fa.org
12 FA Web site www.the-fa.org
13 Phillips-Jones, Linda, *Mentors and Protégés*, Arbor House, New York, 1982.
14 Hill, L.A., 'Developing the star performer', in F. Hesselbein (Editor-in-Chief), *Leader to Leader*, No. 8, Spring 1998 (pp. 30–37), Drucker Foundation, San Francisco, CA.

OPEN GOALS

'*Football in Italy is not all that different from England. One difference is that... I have a very quiet team, like schoolchildren, whereas in Italy the dressing room is very lively, everyone has an opinion and so on. Here at half time, everyone is sitting down, waiting for the manager to talk.*'

– *Sven-Göran Eriksson*[1]

Sven the cosmopolitan

F ootball – like most other sports – has a parochial history. For many years players would play for the team in their home city. Fans would support the local team, and they would rather die than switch allegiance. Even the concept of a team defined in geographical terms – Manchester City, Derby County – is parochial (and very different to the US where sports franchises often hop from city to city). The occasional cases of players moving overseas – Kevin Keegan to Hamburg; the Argentinians Ossie Ardiles and Ricky Villa to Tottenham – were treated as oddities.

Interestingly, the glaring exception to this parochialism is Italy. Foreign players have been welcomed in Italy with open arms for many decades. Italians venerate *calcio* and anyone who can play it well. Foreign players such as the Welshman John Charles became Italian heroes. The Genoa club was even founded by an Englishman and many of its team in the early years of the twentieth century were English. Swedes have similarly thrived – from Gunnar Gren (Milan, Fiorentina and Genoa), Gunnar Nordahl (Milan and Roma), and Nils Liedholm (10 seasons with Milan) – the stars of the 1950s – to Jonas Thern (Napoli and Roma) and Glenn Strömberg (Atalanta Bergamo) in the 1990s.

Football has now opened up, and players, teams, even supporters are international in their outlook. Chelsea famously fielded a starting line-up in 2001 without a single English player on the team. The club's last three managers have been two Italians and a Dutchman. And the Spanish, German and other European leagues are now full of the pick of the talent in Europe and South America.

The reasons for this change are many – the European Champions League which brought the top clubs in Europe together more often, the Bosman ruling that brought free agency to the player market, and of course the enormously lucrative TV deals that are available to the top clubs. Manchester United, Real Madrid and others are now global brands, and they are managed as such by their commercially-minded owners.

But despite this sea-change in the international outlook of football, there is still a split between what sociologists call the 'parochials' and the 'cosmopolitans'. Parochials are inward-focused, concerned primarily about their local community. Cosmopolitans are outward-focused, and gain inspiration in what is happening in the outside world. It manifests itself in obvious things like where you choose to work, live and visit on holiday. But it also manifests itself in more intangible ways, like where your influences come from in fashion, cooking, or sport.

Sven-Göran Eriksson is the archetypal cosmopolitan. He has lived and worked in four countries. And more important, he is energised by the prospect of going wherever in the world the next big challenge lies. He clearly retains an enormous attachment to Sweden – he goes back for his holidays every summer – but he shows no desire to go back there for work.

Many other coaches and players are much more parochial, even if they end up moving overseas. The acid test is what happens *after* that first overseas job. Does the player move back home, yearning for a pint of warm beer and the reruns of *Footballers Wives*? Or does he start soliciting offers from other foreign clubs? Usually it's the former, a sure sign that the player is a parochial at heart.

Why is a cosmopolitan outlook so important? The fact is, no-one has a monopoly on good ideas, and no one country or organisation has a monopoly on good people. So in a global economy, and a highly competitive one to boot, it is dangerous to assume that all the smart people or all the good new ideas come from your corner of the world.

Poor travellers	Cosmopolitan men
Ian Rush: Liverpool hero turned into goal shy novice at Juventus	*Terry Venables*: Successful Barcelona coach
Ron Atkinson: Ex Manchester United manager briefly in charge at Atletico Madrid	*John Toshack*: Moved effortlessly from Swansea in Wales to the Basque country and then Real Madrid
Dennis Bergkamp: Non-flying Dutchman proved a relative failure in Italy	*Kevin Keegan*: European champion at Liverpool converted quickly to the German way at Hamburg
Josef Venglos: Czech manager who didn't travel well to Aston Villa and then Celtic	*Michael Robinson*: Average Liverpool centre forward moved to Spain and became a football commentator
Paul Gascoigne: Lazio wasn't quite ready for Newcastle-style refuelling habits	*Gary Lineker*: English goalscorer who carried on scoring in Spain
Christian Gross: Successful Swiss club manager all at sea at Tottenham	*Glenn Hoddle*: Lagging English career revived by a spell in Monaco
Des Walker: Athletic England defender rendered impotent in Italy	*Tony Woodcock*: English forward who found Germany to his liking

Top football teams now send talent scouts everywhere – not just to Europe and South America, but to Africa and Asia as well. And in the business world Silicon Valley boasts enormous numbers of immigrants from China, India and other countries. Silicon Valley companies like Intel and Sun Microsystems have 'scanning' units in places like Stockholm and Israel to tap into the latest breakthroughs in technology.

A cosmopolitan outlook is best understood as a mindset – as a way of looking at the world. We have talked about the importance of being open to new ways of thinking. Here the emphasis is more on being open to foreign influences, and adapting to different cultural norms. The concept applies at three different levels – the individual, the firm, and the country.

Global leaders

Leaders today need to have a global outlook. New competitors are as likely to emerge from Seoul and Stockholm as from Silicon Valley. Unless the leader understands how such competitors work, he or she is unlikely to react quickly enough. Countless European and American manufacturers – in TVs, white goods, cars and motorbikes – discounted the threat from Japan in the 1960s and 1970s, only to find themselves facing losing out to better and cheaper competing products.

The same rules apply in the football world. The leader has to think globally. The next great talent to illuminate your team is as likely to be playing in the streets of Santiago as Cape Town. Leaders must see the football through the eyes of the world.

According to one survey, the greatest challenge facing successful business leaders over the next five years is technological change (24 per cent), followed by globalisation (18 per cent). To deal with these challenges, the leader will have to embrace change as never before. 'The new leader is one who commits people to action, who converts followers into leaders, and who can convert leaders into agents of change,' says leadership theorist Warren Bennis.[2]

The second challenge facing leaders is that of globalisation. This is a grey area. Business leaders remain enthralled by the American leadership model which is, even now, resolutely North American in style and substance. In a survey carried out by the UK company Impact a staggering 71 per cent professed to believe that the US is currently producing the best leaders in the world. The UK recorded 19 per cent with Germany (7 per cent) and France (a mere 3 per cent) lagging behind.

Clearly, America does not have a monopoly on leadership best practice – though American theorists and commentators tend to suggest otherwise. Truly global leaders require new role models and broader perspectives. These issues are explored by Fons Trompenaars and Charles Hampden-Turner in their book, *21 Leaders for the 21st Century*.

Trompenaars and Hampden-Turner believe that cultural sensitivity is becoming increasingly important for business leaders. 'Basic to understanding other cultures is the awareness that culture is a series of rules and methods that a society has evolved to deal with the recurring problems it faces,' explains Trompenaars. 'They have become so basic that, like breathing, we no longer think about how we approach or resolve them. Every country and every organisation faces dilemmas in relationships with people; dilemmas in relationship to time; and dilemmas in relations between people and the natural environment. Culture is the way in which people resolve dilemmas emerging from universal problems.'[3]

According to this view, successful leaders are adept at reconciling dilemmas. Says Trompenaars: 'We found that the CEOs – people like Jack M. Greenberg of McDonalds; Karel Vuursteen from Heineken; Acer's Stan Shih; Anders Knutsen of Bang and Olufsen; and Club Med's Philippe Bourguignon – typically resolved three or more of our dilemmas.' This requires a degree of organisational and personal flexibility which does not necessarily come easily. Trompenaars points to Shell – 'which has genuinely changed as an organisation' – and McDonald's as examples of sensitivity – 'McDonald's' success has been built through globalising local learning. During the Asian crisis it found it couldn't import potatoes into Malaysia so it re-introduced rice onto the menu. This was a great success so it tried it out elsewhere in the world. It worked'.

Of course, the skills of reconciliation, sensitivity and the like are those commonly – and stereotypically – associated with women leaders. The Impact survey found that women consider themselves to be leaders slightly more than their male counterparts. Even so, there remains a dearth of women business leaders. One problem Trompenaars found in his research was that he had difficulty finding women leaders. He explains: 'First of all, there aren't that many and the first 25 we approached to be interviewed all said that they were too busy. Men said the same but usually relented. The women did not. Our conclusion is that they are less vain. Too bad because they seem to be better reconcilers than men.' The first woman football manager may not be as far away as you might imagine.

The catch to all this is that, at the highest ranks of leadership, most companies are still surprisingly parochial. They want individuals who have broad international experience, but they are also pretty risk-averse and typically plump for the home-grown executive rather than the foreigner. Run your eye down a list of the biggest companies in the US, Japan, France, Italy or Germany, and you will only find a handful of foreigners – Carlos Ghosn at Nissan, the Swede Lars Nyberg at NCR. British companies are unusual in their openness to foreign executives, as we discuss below. Sweden is mixed – the top executives are mostly the old guard, typically fairly cosmopolitan in outlook but still very Swedish. But there are also some foreign CEOs, such as Italian-born Giulio Mazzalupi at Atlas Copco.

But even if most leaders are still born-and-bred locals, there are signs that this is changing. AnnaLee Saxenian, a professor at University of California, Berkeley, has examined the role played by Chinese and Indian immigrants in the growth of Silicon Valley. She discovered that many of the big success stories like Yahoo!, Sun, and eBay were founded by immigrants who were attracted by the endless opportunities California seemed to offer. But more important, she observes, some are now heading back home to Asia, to start up new businesses and to encourage others to do the same. Rather than worrying about a brain drain out of Asia, she argues that there is increasing evidence of a 'brain circulation' between countries which benefits all of them.

Think global; act global

How cosmopolitan is your organisation? Here there is a lot of variation, even within the same sectors. Some companies are highly international in their sales, but parochial in their overall way of working. Examples are Japanese companies like Hitachi and Matsushita, American companies Caterpillar, Boeing, and AT&T, Germany companies like Thyssen Krupp and Allianz. Others are becoming less parochial as they recognise the benefits of a more global outlook – DaimlerChrysler, GE, and Sony. Such companies are, for example, now requiring executives to spend some time overseas before they can be considered for top leadership positions. And there are a few companies that have been truly cosmopolitan for many years – ABB, Novartis, and Schlumberger for example.

When it comes to producing cosmopolitan companies, Sweden is remarkably successful – the only worthwhile European comparisons are with Switzerland and the Netherlands. Its companies transcend boundaries in ways few others can manage. Internationalisation is in the Swedish genes. Exports account for 40 per cent of Sweden's GDP. Transfers to foreign subsidiaries have long been regarded as important learning opportunities rather than demotions. Many Swedes end up spending decades overseas, though most return home sooner or later.

The international success of Swedish business is exemplified by the unlikely example of a company which exercised a monopoly for most of the twentieth century and remains state owned. When its monopoly was finally lifted 300 competitors flocked to the market. You would expect the company to have been consigned to history. Instead it now owns one of the biggest brands in the world. Sweden's Vin & Sprit (V&S) is the state-owned success story and Absolut its star brand. The winner from Absolut's global success is the Swedish government – in 1999 V&S brought in SEK 230 million ($25 million) – the very same government which has one of the most restrictive alcohol policies in Europe.

V&S has succeeded largely because of its commitment to being different. State-owned monopolists are not usually renowned for their capacity to take risks or be imaginative and innovative in any way. V&S has. Its ad campaigns and the clever extensions to the Absolut brand have cemented its reputation for shrewd brand stewardship.

Analysing the brand's international success, CEO Göran Lundqvist suggests that there is no blueprint, but believes that the major element is that Absolut considers the United States as its home market. 'Perhaps that's the secret. Sweden is where we manufacture and make decisions, but we grow from the US out into the world,' he says. 'To do so, you need an information network and research that keep you abreast of what's happening in the market. You have to be very local when you speak to consumers. You have to understand the market and respect the consumers in the market. We treat all of our consumers with respect.'[4]

Lundqvist was a Ohio State undergraduate and is naturally international, in the mould of so many Swedish executives. It is, he says, a force of geography and culture: 'No-one speaks Swedish. No-one knows our culture. We're forced to adapt. We're a very small market – just 9 million people – with a high level of education. It's a state of mind. The Dutch are the same. As a result, we find it easy to work in the United States. It is very straightforward and uncomplicated. They are also interested in the end results. It is just that our idols are different.'

Sweden and the other Scandinavian countries have to embrace the world because the world is unlikely to rush towards the North Pole to embrace them. Small home markets offer strong incentives to internationalise. And internationalise they have. 'With our high dependency on trade, we have become open to influences from elsewhere. There is a feeling that we don't belong and this means that we can pick the best ideas no matter where they come from,' says Jan Lapidoth. 'The lesson from Scandinavia is simple: leave home. Leave your home market. Pit your wits against the best in the world and open your mind as your markets are opened. Don't blame the Japanese for ruining your car making. The US is very big but the world is bigger.'

Swedish open

Countries exhibit very different levels of openness to foreign influences and ideas. Sweden has a long tradition of openness. A wave of Dutch immigrants in the 1600s was responsible for founding the city of Gothenburg, and it was subsequently developed in the 1700s by Scottish and English immigrants. The Swedish steel, pulp and paper, and textiles industries were developed in the 1800s through the efforts

of German and French immigrants. Many of Sweden's most successful entrepreneurs got their ideas from abroad. Lars Magnus Ericsson
worked at the Siemens telegraph equipment plant in Germany before
starting his own company in Stockholm. Jonas Alströmer got inspiration from England before founding the first Swedish textile mill.

Despite these early influences, Sweden also had its dark ages
in the middle part of the twentieth century. Convinced of the direct
effect of outward investment on Swedish wealth, the Social Demo-
cratic government brought in strict controls on foreign ownership of
Swedish companies, and they made it difficult for foreigners to work
in Sweden. For many decades television in Sweden was heavily regulated, with imported shows from the UK and the US strictly rationed.
Sweden, like Britain, was a late entrant into the European Community,
and as we write is still adamantly opposed to the Euro.

Today Sweden is one of the most open countries in the world,
and Sven-Göran Eriksson is just one of many Swedes who has built a
successful international career. The reasons are as much to do with attitude as government regulations. All Swedes learn English from a very
young age, and many spend a year in school in the UK or the US. Cable
television, mostly from the US, is left in its English-language form with
subtitles (unlike in most of Europe where it is dubbed). The younger
generation are keen to work abroad, with London the number one
destination. Their appetite for new technologies and new fashions is
second to none. No surprise, then, that Swedes make such effective
global managers. Lars Nyberg is the CEO of NCR, a major American IT
company. Anders Moberg was headhunted from IKEA by American
retailer Home Depot to run its international operations. Companies
like IKEA, Tetra Pak and Ericsson have been sending Swedes overseas
to run their foreign affiliates for decades. No less an authority than Jack
Welch has also praised the Swedes. He commented to the *Financial
Times* in 1997, 'We are trying desperately to hire more global people.
There are certain people who are more comfortable in global environ-
ments. The Dutch, the Swedes … A Swede is a global traveller.'

The ambivalent Englishman

Britain shares a lot more with Sweden on this issue than an aversion
to joining the Eurozone. In fact, like Swedes, British people exhibit

a highly schizophrenic quality when it comes to opening itself up to foreign influences. They condemn most European initiatives, they worry about the threat to their sovereignty, and they grumble about the creeping influence of Brussels and the Euro over their daily lives. But at the same time Britain is actually one of the most open countries in Europe. Consider a few interesting and eclectic examples:

- **Foreign trade and foreign investment.** The British Isles has always been the first point of entry for American and Japanese companies entering Europe, and today Britain still gets the lion's share of investment. The result is that some industries – automobiles, computers, semiconductors – are almost exclusively foreign owned today. And this is not necessarily a bad thing. Take a look at the investment banks in London – once-proud British merchant banks like Morgan Grenfell, Hill Samuel, and Samuel Montagu have all been bought up by foreign competitors. The ultimate decision makers may be overseas, but the real value-added work is all done in London. And the Square Mile has never been stronger.

- **Food.** English cuisine has been the butt of foreign jokes for longer than anyone cares to remember. But even the French are finally starting to wise up to the fact that Britain has some great chefs and some great restaurants. And if you want a good curry or a good Chinese meal, you could do a lot worse than visit Bradford or Manchester. Why this turnaround in Britain's culinary fortunes? Partly because the country has embraced all things foreign. Britain does not have a noble heritage to live up to, so it has created its own version of the American melting pot.

- **Language.** Compare the English language to French. English gets stretched, modified, and abused. It is forever changing, as new expressions and words get picked up and assimilated from America, Germany, France, even Sweden. Most multinational companies have now adopted English as their working language, but as Percy Barnevik the former CEO of ABB has acknowledged, 'we don't speak English, we speak broken English'. Linguists, apparently, have noted that English is the easiest language to speak badly. Compare this to French, which is protected by *l'Académie*

Française like an endangered species. The Academie decides what changes – if any – will be allowed to the French language. It creates new words when the American equivalent is deemed too gauche. And the French language is slowly but surely losing its influence on the world stage. Two years ago, the number of EU documents published in English finally exceeded the number in French, a true watershed.

- **Management.** British businesspeople have finally figured out that good managers do not have to come from within their boundaries. Richard Giordano of BOC was an early example. Now there are plenty of foreigners leading top British companies – Ben Verwaayen at BT, Luc Vandevelde at M&S, Marjorie Scardino at Pearson, JP Garnier at GSK, and Matthew Barrett at Barclays Bank.

The underlying point is simple. In a world of interlinked economies, no country is an island. Sweden figured this out some time ago, as did

Sven yourself

- How many countries have you lived in?
- How many languages do you speak?
- How many nationalities are there in the team or group you work closely with?
- When you go abroad on holiday, do you 'go native' or do you stick to the tourist shopping areas and the tourist hotels?
- How cosmopolitan is your company?
- What percentage of your sales are overseas? How many of your manufacturing, R&D and sales units are overseas?
- Do you know what's happening in competitors' home markets?
- What are the nationalities of your top executives and board of directors?
- Where do executive and board meetings take place?
- Where do the decision makers in your business units and functional areas work?
- Do you provide equal opportunities for locals and foreigners?
- Are expatriate assignments seen as a punishment or reward?
- How many senior execs have done an international tour of duty?

the Netherlands. Britain seems to be getting there. Interestingly, many other countries still try to keep the walls up around many aspects of their economy. Remember the shock in 2000 when German company Mannesman surrendered to a hostile takeover bid by the British company Vodafone. Or the bizarre acquisition in 2001 of Olivetti by Pirelli, the sole purpose of which seemed to be to ensure that the company stayed in Italian hands. Japan is the worst offender – a country whose economy has been going backwards for the best part of a decade, but with the glaring exception of Nissan – which has allowed Renault to sort out its problems – its large companies have shown no interest in applying the laws of restructuring that Europe and America figured out long ago.

Notes

1 Interview with George Yip, London Business School, 28 September 2001.
2 Author interview.
3 Author interview.
4 Author interview.

12

FACE UP TO FAILURE

'If you have been doing a job for 20 years without ever feeling like you failed you are either a very happy man or a little bit stupid.'

Sven-Göran Eriksson[1]

Fail to succeed

Being an executive is all about achieving great results; succeeding by whatever measure is fashionable, relevant or used by your employer. Executives need success to move up the corporate ladder. This, at least, is the received wisdom on executive life. More fashionable theories, however, suggest that failure is the route to real long-lasting success. California, the hot-bed of the new economy, leads the charts when it comes to business failures. In the fevered entrepreneurial world of e-business, venture capitalists are looking for people who are prepared to stick their necks out and take risks. And taking risks will, inevitably, bring failures.

Failure is increasingly recognised as an essential part of personal and professional development because, simply, it provides learning. 'Because many professionals are almost always successful at what they do, they rarely experience failure. And because they have rarely failed, they have never learned how to learn from failure,' says Harvard Business School's Chris Argyris.

In search of risk-taking failures who learn as they go along, companies are taking a variety of initiatives. The most obvious move is to reward and recognise failures. The CEO of a major US corporation caused a furore at his senior executive forum by handing out awards for Best Failures.

At a practical level, how people react when things go wrong is critical to their ability to do their job. This is usually overlooked. If you start a job on the checkout counter of a retail chain, you will spend a day watching videos (it's cheap and doesn't waste valuable managerial time) about the way the corporation works, its values and ways of doing things. This does not prepare people to deal with what happens when things go wrong – because if things go wrong they are fired. Another retail chain has a better idea. It throws staff in at the deep end by giving them a day at the counter to see how they deal with real customers. Then it can make a decision about whether someone is really right for the job.

Failure is inextricably linked to risk. Work at Decision Research, a company based in Eugene, Oregon, studying risk management strategies, suggests that people are more likely to accept risks that they perceive as voluntarily undertaken, controllable, understandable and equally distributed. And, conversely, people are less willing to take on risks which they don't understand and which are unfairly distributed.

'Share, understand and confront – then risks, even if they fail, can become learning,' advise leadership theorists Randall White and Philip Hodgson, authors of *Relax, It's Only Uncertainty*. Take Disney's initially disastrous venture into Europe. Given the size of its losses, it was undoubtedly tempting for Disney executives to sweep the matter under the corporate carpet and attempt as much as possible to forget about it. Instead, Disney executives recall its lessons every day. 'Euro Disney gave us all a good glass of cold water to the face,' admitted Michael Eisner. 'There's not a meeting goes by that somebody doesn't say, 'Ah, Euro Disney, Euro Disney. Can we afford to do this?' Okay, I've heard it. I can say we've learned. But I really do feel – about business and about life – that everybody has to make mistakes, it's okay. I have never wavered from the belief that I'm glad we did Euro Disney and that it is a monument to the creativity of our company.'[2]

'Fear of failure has to give way to respect for failure and learning from failure. Executives need to toughen up. They are going to be tested and tested again in ways they never previously contemplated. This takes humility and bravura,' advise White and Hodgson. 'Building from failure tests executive resilience. Our work with derailed executives found, not surprisingly, that all executives make mistakes. At senior levels these mistakes could be costly, capital intensive ones. The crucial thing was that when the successful executives make mistakes they acknowledged and accepted them. The derailed, however, rejected them, often blaming others. The resilient executive takes in experiences, particularly failures, and incorporates them into a structure of concepts that is used to evaluate future experience and guide future actions. Resilient executives learn from experiences, both good and bad.'

Jim Collins, the American author of *Good to Great* makes a similar observation. He talks in terms of 'the window and the mirror'. Great leaders, he argues, look out the window to apportion credit – they acknowledge colleagues, and they admit to a fair dose of good luck. But they look in the mirror to assign responsibility – they never blame outside events when things go wrong. Leaders of less-successful companies, by contrast, tend to do the opposite – they look out the window for factors to blame, but they gaze in the mirror to credit themselves when things go well.

Ericsson shows an impressive ability to learn from its mistakes. Its mobile handset business – which at one point was equal market leader with Nokia – was officially killed off several times when it was first being developed in the late 1980s. Fortunately for Ericsson the guy behind it, Åke Lundqvist, did not accept 'no' for an answer. He moved his operation to southern Sweden, away from head office, and he kept going until he could prove the viability of the product. The learning within the company is clear – give new technologies time and space to succeed, because you never know where the next blockbuster product will come from.

The true measure of any leader is their response to failure. Failure is good for you. When life gives you lemons, make lemonade.

Making the most of failure

Despite the silverware dotted around his resume, Eriksson has also faced criticism and failure from time to time. 'I have been at a good school for the last few years in Italy where it's not easy when things go badly. It will be the biggest challenge so far in my life,' noted Eriksson on his appointment to the England job.[3]

At Gothenburg he totally changed the team's approach to playing the game. Instead of a somewhat cavalier attacking game, the team adopted a stricter 4–4-2 pattern with an emphasis on getting the ball forward quickly. It was relatively unsophisticated. Fans campaigned at Gothenburg to have him removed and the players even voted on whether Eriksson should stay after he offered to resign following some particularly vituperative criticism. They backed him.

'I was not impressed. He was not very tall and he looked like nothing. I thought "Is he going to take over this big club?" We played with a libero and he changed that. The first couple of games we didn't play too well. There was a lot of criticism and after four games we were bottom of the league. We had a meeting and he said: "If you don't want me to continue, I'll go",'[4] says Glenn Hysén who played under Eriksson at Gothenburg. Eriksson survived and emerged victorious. (In November 2001 when Eriksson was named as Sweden's football personality of the year, he received the award from the 1982 Gothenburg team with whom he won the UEFA Cup.)

Making the most of failure requires that you:

- **Bounce back.** Good leaders have high self-awareness. Once the initial disappointment of defeat or failure has worn off, they reflect on what went wrong, and they are able to dispassionately analyse where the problems arose. Changes are made, and quickly the leader is energising his or her team towards the next challenge. A great example of this comes from Rank Xerox, the European arm of the American copier company. In 1995 it launched a major growth initiative in Europe led by Carlos Camarero. Wave I was a great success, but Wave II failed miserably. But rather than give up in despair, or blame outside events, Camarero analysed where Wave II had failed, and quickly introduced a Wave III (even though it had not been planned). It succeeded, and Camarero's reputation was saved.[5]
- **Never punish honest failure.** Everyone understands the argument that you have to accept well-intentioned failure as part of the development of new products and new ways of working. But translating that logic into practice is a very different story. One executive we interviewed at a leading UK company commented that 'There are actually no examples here where people failed to meet their goals and were still rewarded'. And this is far from unusual. Companies talk about the importance of meeting targets, or the 'zero tolerance' for error, on the basis that this provides the discipline needed for success. But the sort of success it breeds is risk-averse and incremental. If you want true radical innovation, or breakthrough growth, you need to celebrate and even encourage honest failure.
- **Admit it when you're wrong.** According to Jim Collins, one of the key attributes of so-called Level Five leaders is humility. This manifests itself in an ability to own up to your own mistakes. It is always possible to find some external factor to blame when things go wrong. Just think back to the number of companies who rushed out profit warnings in the wake of the September 11th atrocities. Some, like the airlines and the insurance companies, had good reason to blame the events of that day, but many others showed more tenuous reasoning.

  Ericsson again is an interesting example. While the story has never been widely publicised, it is common knowledge within the company that a small fortune was spent on a new digital switch called AXE-N between 1989 and 1995. AXE-N was an integrated next-generation switch, but it proved to be too big and unwieldy and it never took off. The company wrote off the entire investment – a clear acknowledgement that they got it wrong. And more to the point, they learned from this failure by moving towards a more modularised and open-system approach to technology development.

- **Learn from failure.** Failure is the best source of feedback. Sven-Göran Eriksson probably learns more from watching England lose than from watching them win. He can figure out which players respond well under pressure, and which ones lose heart. He can analyse where attacking moves broke down, and where the gaps in defence opened up. In the business world, losing a major bid or watching a new product flop can offer enormous insights into where problems lie – as long as you are prepared to accept responsibility for the mistake and analyse how it arose.

Compare this to the challenge facing Airbus as it designs its new 600-seater plane. The hope and intention is that this plane will never fall out of the sky. The whole design process has to be done on the basis of computer simulations, and by extrapolating from the problems experienced by other planes. There is no opportunity to learn directly from failure.

Failure has its benefits, but it is also expensive. The best way of reconciling these two points is to make small bets. Risk taking need not be a big single bet on one outcome. It can involve a more calculated process of experimentation in which a small investment is made and then evaluated. If it works out, a larger investment is made. If it does not, only a small amount is lost. This is how venture capitalists work, and it is a proven way of maximising the up-side while managing the down-side risk.

Percy Barnevik, former CEO of ABB, expresses the same point slightly differently. 'Nothing is worse than procrastination' he says. 'When I look at ten decisions I regret, there will be nine of them where I delayed. Better roughly and quickly than carefully and slowly'. Barnevik espouses a 7–3 formula, which reinforces the notion that it is better to make decisions quickly and be right seven out of ten times than to waste time trying to achieve the perfect solution. 'The only thing we cannot accept is people who make no decision' he says.[6]

Postscript

Sweden's greatest footballing success came in the 1958 World Cup. Helped by home advantage, as England were in 1966, the Swedes reached the final only to be beaten by Brazil (featuring the 17-year old Pele and Garrincha). At the time the Swedish team was coached by the unlikeliest of heroes, an Englishman called George Raynor. The parallels, in reverse, with Sven-Göran Eriksson are irresistible.

Raynor was a small Yorkshireman born in 1907. The son of a miner, he played for lower league English teams including Sheffield United, Mansfield, Bury and Rotherham. His career was unexceptional. After World War II he was to be found coaching British soldiers in Baghdad. Then the FA requested that he go to Sweden to help the Swedes out. Raynor became Sweden's coach in 1946.

Raynor advocated a more subtle and skilful game than his background in the lower leagues of English football might have suggested. 'Control the ball, then let it do the work for you like a dance – slow, slow, quick-quick, slow.' Under Raynor, Sweden played an early form of possession football.

It worked. He coached Sweden to the Olympic gold medal in 1948 when the Swedes overcame Denmark and Czechoslovakia to win at Wembley. Defending their gold in Helsinki, the Swedes came third. He went on to coach them in the 1950 and 1958 World Cups. In 1950 in Uruguay they came third. One of the team's stars – unearthed by Raynor in his travels around Sweden – was Hasse Jeppson who later played in Italy with Atalanta and Napoli. Though they didn't qualify for the 1954 finals, in 1958 Sweden progressed until they met Brazil in a thrilling final which Brazil eventually won. Raynor was honoured by the King of Sweden.

The Swedish team under Raynor had a trio of stars: Gunnar Gren, Gunnar Nordahl and Niels Liedholm – known collectively as Gre-no-li. They eventually left Sweden to star at Milan where they scored 329 goals between them.

In 1959 Sweden travelled to Wembley to beat England 3–2. It was George Raynor's crowning glory.

After that Raynor headed home. It seemed he had made his point. He had built up a virtually unknown football nation into one of the best in the world playing a new brand of possession football.

In a bizarre link to Sven-Göran Eriksson, Raynor was briefly coach of Lazio in 1954–5 when Lazio finished 12th in Serie A. Raynor's record at Lazio was played 28, won 10, drew 7, and lost 11, giving an average of 1.06 points per game. Eriksson's record at Lazio was played 188, won 106, drew 48, lost 34 giving an average of 1.38 points per game.

In the UK, George Raynor was ignored rather than fêted. He was briefly at Coventry City. Then, slowly slipping down the leagues, Raynor spent time at Doncaster Rovers. Eventually, his glories were well and truly put behind him and Raynor finished up working as a storeman at the Butlin's holiday camp in the English resort of Skegness where he was also honorary manager of Skegness Town. Sven-Göran Eriksson certainly knows of Raynor's heroic achievements with the Swedish team. It would be interesting to know how much he knows about the rest of Raynor's career.

Notes

1 Anthony, Andrew, 'Svengland', *The Observer*, 5 August 2001.
2 Author interview.
3 'Up to the job', http://sportsillustrated.cnn.com, November 2 2000.
4 Anthony, Andrew, 'Svengland', *The Observer*, 5 August 2001.
5 This story is taken from 'Rank Xerox Team C' case study, Gabriel Szulanski, Wharton School of Management, 1997.
6 These quotes drawn from Asea Brown Boveri case, Harvard Business School 9-192-139, by C.A. Bartlett.

INDEX